THE PRACTICAL ANGLER

TOGETHER WITH

A CAUTION TO ANGLERS

W.C. Stewart (standing) with angling companion.

THE

PRACTICAL ANGLER

OR

THE ART OF TROUT-FISHING

MORE PARTICULARLY APPLIED TO CLEAR WATER

TOGETHER WITH

A CAUTION TO ANGLERS

BY

W. C. STEWART

The Fly Fishers Classic Library
2009

THE PRACTICAL ANGLER

First published by A & C Black in 1857
Reissued with new introduction & coloured plates in 1905

A CAUTION TO ANGLERS

First published by A & C Black in 1871

In 1996 The Flyfisher's Classic Library
published an edition of 500 copies of The Practical Angler,
taken from the 1905 edition, but omitting the colour plates

This combined edition with new colour plates is published by
The Flyfisher's Classic Library in 2009
Also published by Coch-y-Bonddu Books Ltd in paperback 2009

Introductory material © Conrad Voss Bark 1995 & Richard Hunter 2009
New plates of flies tied and photographed by Terry Griffiths 2009

This book is from an edition limited to 500 copies
plus a de luxe edition of only 50 copies

© 2009 The Flyfisher's Classic Library
An imprint of
Coch-y-Bonddu Books Ltd, Machynlleth, Powys SY20 8DG
01654 702837

www.ffcl.com   www.anglebooks.com

ISBN 978 1 905396 05 4

All rights reserved.
No part of this publication may be reproduced,
stored in a retrieval system, or transmitted, in any form
or by any means, electronic, mechanical, photocopying,
recording or otherwise, without the prior consent
of the copyright holder.

CONTENTS

The Spread of a Great Idea vi
William Clouston Stewart: A Biographical Note ix
The Late Mr Stewart xxi
Author's Preface xxiii
1905 Contents page..xxvii
1905 Introduction by W. Earl Hodgson xxxi
Introduction to colour fly plates by Terry Griffiths xliii
Book of Flies for Loch & Stream xliv
The Practical Angler 1
Index 227
Introduction to A Caution to Anglers by Richard Hunter ..229
A Caution to Anglers...233

Stewart

The Spread of a Great Idea

———◆———

WHEN I was a boy, fishing the Yorkshire becks for the wild trout of the wolds it seemed natural to me to cast my flies down-stream to attract the trout by the way the flies would flicker and lift and move with the movements of the current. But one day an old man who had been watching me for some time came across and with the natural courtesy of the countryman told me that a better way to take a trout was to fish my flies upstream and across.

"Coming from behind the fish you'll not scare them. You'll hook them better. Make short casts. Like this, if you don't mind." He took my greenheart rod and cast beautifully into the quiet places behind rocks, into the curls of water and the runnels under the bank. "Search for the fish," he went on. "Let your flies drift no more than a couple of yards, lift off, and cast again further up. Always searching. Don't matter if your flies sink a bit but the best time for a take is when they first fall on the water."

It was pure Stewart though I didn't know that at the time and whether he had read *The Practical Angler* was unlikely, but great ideas have an infectious way of spreading beyond the printed page. Written in the 1850s the book was years ahead of its contemporaries. It put the case for fishing the fly upstream and across with a precision, clarity, and a minute attention to detail which had never been known before. It was the first of its kind. Edition after edition was sold out. He was years ahead of the chalk stream purists of the south which maybe is why Halford and Francis were both a little contemptuous of this Border fisherman, this wet fly angler. But for the far greater number of flyfishers on the limestone and spate rivers of England and Scotland he had created a firm tradition, passed on by later writers, such as Pritt and Walbran, Edmonds and Lee, which triumphantly survives.

Not only has the book good practical advice but is written - and this is rare in angling literature - with a pervasive charm and vivid choice of words that takes you effortlessly to the rivers that he loved. Some of the images he conjures up - James Baillie of an earlier generation of Border anglers with his hazel rod and a length of string tied to the top - are unforgettable. In these ways, and in many others, when you come to read Stewart you come to have an affection for him.

He knew little or nothing of entomology, and did

not pretend to, all the same his fly patterns, based on those of James Baillie and perhaps even anglers of earlier generations, give the impression, the flickering illusion, of living insects swirled and struggling in the tumbled currents of fast moorland rivers. Not long ago I went into a tobacconist's shop in Jedburgh on the Borders on my way to fish Jed Water and there were Stewart's flies, his spider patterns, all ready for me in their little boxes. He was a great man was Stewart. I wish I'd known him.

Conrad Voss Bark
Devon 1995

William Clouston Stewart

A Biographical Note

—◆—

THE *Practical Angler or the Art of Trout Fishing more particularly applied to clear water*, first published in 1857, is the most accomplished and significant trout angling work ever written by a Scotsman.

John Waller Hills, Arnold Gingrich, James Robb and Conrad Voss Bark all acknowledge the remarkable contribution of this benchmark book to the history of angling. From its definitive description of the merits of upstream casting to the thoroughly sensible advocation of "light stiff rods" and "fine thin gut", from the assertion of the "necessity of avoiding bulky flies" to the lucid explanation of upstream low water worming the book displays a depth of knowledge of the craft, and a passion for the sport of angling few have matched and even fewer surpassed. And yet, from the time of the first publication of *The Practical Angler* to the most recent centenary edition of 1957 the author has only been afforded the almost anonymous appellation "W. C. Stewart".

A BIOGRAPHICAL NOTE

If *The Practical Angler* was simply a mundane anecdotal resume of one man's angling reminiscences rather than a cogent guide to the ethos and techniques of fly fishing for trout in clear fast flowing waters, the obscurity of the author would be of import and concern to no-one.

However, the historic impact and continuing validity of much of this thoughtful, sensible and authoritative book has been recognized since its first appearance. To illuminate something of the man behind the text was a task long overdue and by fortune, perseverance, and with much kind assistance I have been able to shed a little light upon the life of this distinguished Victorian angler.

Quite the most remarkable and unexpected result of my enquiries has been the revelation that *The Practical Angler* was written by William Clouston Stewart when he was a mere 24 years of age. The maturity of the content of the book may indeed owe much to the memory of James Baillie, the angling and writing of those such as John Younger and Thomas Tod Stoddart as well as the editorial skills of Alexander Russel, but even so, there can have been very few readers who would have credited an author of such youth.

To put his achievement in some kind of perspective, it should be noted that Viscount Grey was 36 when *Fly Fishing* appeared in 1899, G. E. M. Skues was 52 when *The Minor Tactics of the Chalk Stream* was published in 1910, and William Scrope was all of 70 when he wrote his classic *Days and Nights of Salmon Fishing on the Tweed*.

"W. C." was evidently a very keen angler, but that he had amassed the experience drawn upon in this book and distilled the essentials of his particular art in such an assured and informative volume is testimony to his special place in the history of the literature of angling.

The life of William Clouston Stewart began on the third of June 1832, five years before the accession of Victoria and the year of Sir Walter Scott's death. He was born in a small cul-de-sac off Leith Walk, a location today encompassed by the City of Edinburgh but that was then within the soon-to-become fully independent burgh of Leith. (Leith was absorbed into the larger Royal Burgh as recently as 1920 so it is only accurate to refer to him as a "Leither" rather than a son of the City of Edinburgh.) His parents William Stewart and Jean Clouston were both native Orcadians who had married in the town of Stromness, Orkney, in December 1827.

It is tempting to contemplate that the superb trout fishing of Orkney and the continuing fine tradition of its anglers may have contributed in some measure to William Clouston's innate angling skills but as yet there is no evidence to suggest he stayed in Orkney, although with his grandparents resident in the isles and having a relatively prosperous father, it is by no means improbable that he may have cast a line on some of the Orkney islands' productive waters.

Following their marriage, the Stewarts settled initially in Leith, a thriving port, where William set himself up as a wholesale merchant. Their first child was named after his paternal Orcadian grandfather, but it is upon the birth of their second son in 1832 that the name of William Clouston Stewart is recorded in South Leith Parish Register. Not long afterwards, William Stewart senior relocated his business and family in the rapidly developing city of Dundee, trading as a wine and spirit merchant. One rather intriguing fact concerning William Clouston Stewart is that at the age of nine he was not resident in the family home when the 1841 census enumerator visited 18 Seafield Lane, Dundee. History does not at present relate a reason for this absence and until an index to the 1841 census is compiled, young William's whereabouts shall remain unexplained.

At this juncture the family life of young William Stewart and his brothers, Balfour, Edward and his only sister, Isabella, was surely greatly disturbed by the death of their mother at the age of 46 in 1841. With a young family and a small merchant business to nurture, William Stewart senior had practical domestic considerations as well as the evident emotional reasons to marry again, so it is not surprising that in

March 1843, Georgina Anderson, the daughter of a Sutherland farmer, became his second wife.

For the next five years it seems the Stewart household remained in Dundee but between the years of 1848, when William Stewart senior ceased to be a wine merchant, and 1858 when he reappears as an established commission agent and merchant in Edinburgh, there is regrettably little documentary evidence to trace the life of his angling son.

Given the extent and nature of the angling experience drawn upon for *The Practical Angler* it is obvious that much of young Stewart's life between the age of 16 and publication of the book in 1857 was spent in Edinburgh, East Lothian and the Border hinterland. One should bear in mind his own testimony in the original preface where he states that "for more than fifteen years we have pursued angling with the greatest assiduity". This diligence was practised in spite of a debilitating fever "W. C." suffered when he was approximately twenty years old, an illness that seemingly had a permanently adverse effect on his constitution. Nonetheless, in the succeeding four years he managed to embark upon a career in commerce, indulge his passion for angling and conceive and write *The Practical Angler*.

One year and three further editions after this book was published, and so warmly received, as the reviews in *The Field*, *The Scotsman* and *Bells Life in London* illustrate, one can fairly readily establish the fortune of the various members of the Stewart household. William Clouston and his surviving brother Edward, both of whom were destined to remain bachelors, had joined their father as wholesale tea merchants. Their elder sister, Isabella, was about to marry a Liverpool merchant with the singularly Orcadian surname of Flett, and the Stewart family were living in the house, at 5 Alva Street, Edinburgh that William Clouston was to inhabit for the remainder of his life.

Although William C. Stewart, his father and stepmother were "away on holiday in England" when the 1861 census was taken, and no more information can be gleaned from that historical source, the by now well-kent angler and author was recommended and duly elected as a member of the Edinburgh Angling Club on the seventh of February 1861. The extant minutes of this fine organization, whilst not comprehensive, do shed a little more light upon William C. Stewart the angler. Concurrent with his election to the Committee in 1862, the Club instituted an annual trout fishing match to be conducted on, (Rule 2) "any part of any unpreserved stream", employing (Rule 6) "any kind of lure except salmon roe". Our distinguished author could only tie for second place in the inaugural contest, the winner being Alexander Russel (Scotsman editor and author of *The Salmon*, 1864) but William Clouston Stewart duly carried off the first prize in

1863. Curiously, at this juncture, at the same meeting confirming his appointment as Secretary and Treasurer to the Edinburgh Angling Club, William Stewart seconded a motion to discontinue this annual trout competition. It was only in 1867 that the Club reintroduced a trout angling contest to be held at Loch Leven. Since Stewart patently thought fishing in still water a poor substitute for the Southern streams his involvement in this process is somewhat puzzling. Whatever his reasoning, of the six subsequent angling competitions at Scotland's premier still water, W. C. Stewart won three and tied for the victor's laurel in another. His efforts in Edinburgh Angling Club's annual salmon angling event for the President's medal, normally conducted on the River Tweed in November, were not as successful, with only one triumph in eight outings. This may suggest that William C. Stewart's proposed text on salmon angling, publicised by A & C Black in the 1867 edition of *The Practical Angler* as the companion volume, might not have been its equal. What stage in the publication process Stewart's proposed volume reached we shall never know since no trace of it remains and Adam and Charles Black's records contain no indication of its ultimate fate. Should by some chance any vestige of the book indeed survive it would be a most unusual and valuable item.

The only other known "Stewart" publication is

A Caution to Anglers, a booklet occasioned by, and engrossing most of the letters exchanged between Stewart and Cholmondley Pennell on the subject of the contrary woolliness of the latter's *The Modern Practical Angler*. Cholmondley Pennell's book from its misnomer of a title to its downstream angling theorizing deeply affronted William C. Stewart's upstream angling principles and his riposte is a delightfully forthright demolition of his rival's postulations. *A Caution to Anglers* was published in 1871 yet within a year the Edinburgh Angling Club had lost its foremost exponent.

William Clouston Stewart died on the seventeenth of January 1872, aged only 40. His final unpleasant illness was occasioned by a month of influenza compounded by an attack of confluent smallpox.

Although Victorian press obituaries are not characterized by their restraint or understatement, the testimonial of *The Scotsman* of the eighteenth of January was sincere and effusive in its praise of the man and the angler:

> "William Stewart was one of the truest, tenderest, kindest of God's creatures. His gentle, anxious aid in sickness; his earnest and thoughtful sympathy in sorrow; his joyous cordial companionship in hours of ease—alike made him as a brother to a host of friends. Far beyond the circle of private friends, he was known as an angler of almost miraculous skill, and as the author of a book which may be said to have

revolutionised the art of trout fishing."

The article remarks upon his proficiency in curling, bowling and indoor games of skill or calculation.

That Stewart enjoyed such pursuits is confirmed by a *Fishing Gazette* article of 1890, penned by "Helvellyn", that gives the following anonymous account of "the Long Un" as Stewart was reportedly cried by his intimates.

> " ... although Stewart was absorbed in his pursuit at the waterside, at the close of the day he was often very animated. He was an easy and lively talker, with a keen relish for a joke, and he took as much delight in a rubber of whist as in fishing. While angling he seemed to possess something like the influence of a fish charmer over the trout.
>
> "I have seen him, without any attempt to conceal his tall figure, plunging and splashing in the Clyde, in a way that would have frightened away every trout within fifty yards, if he had been an ordinary angler, and yet hooking a trout at almost every cast. Curiously enough on this occasion, he was fishing downstream in comparatively clear water."

This article includes a photograph naming Stewart that allowed the positive identification of the frontispiece to this edition.

William Clouston Stewart was laid to rest on the nineteenth of January 1872 in Dean Cemetery, one of Edinburgh's finest private burial grounds. His grave is marked, and his life remembered by a fine red granite monument erected at the behest of his father:

The stone has no embellishment or further inscription despite the oft-quoted Edinburgh Angling epithet, which Stewart may have enjoyed if not quite approved of: "Our secretary Stewart, the King of Anglers he."

It therefore remains his book, *The Practical Angler or The Art of Trout Fishing more particularly applied to clear water*, that survives as his epitaph. A classic of angling literature of enduring quality and relevance, written by an intelligent, perceptive and spirited Scotsman who seems to have been from all that is known of him, as fine an individual as he was an angler and author.

Richard Hunter
Perth, 1995

The Tweed

THE LATE MR. W. C. STEWART.

The Author of this volume died, aged 40, on the 17th of January 1872. The following appeared in the *Scotsman* of the next morning :—

"It is peculiarly painful to us to announce, as it will be to a various and widely-scattered multitude to learn, that this excellent and well-loved man has gone from among us. It will make a great difference to a great many people. William Stewart was one of the truest, tenderest, kindest, of God's creatures. His gentle, anxious aid in sickness; his earnest and thoughtful sympathy in sorrow; his joyous cordial companionship in hours of ease—alike made him as a brother to a host of friends. Far beyond the circle of private friends he was known as an angler of almost miraculous skill, and as the author of a book which may be said to have revolutionised the art of trout-fishing. His skill as an angler was indeed unsurpassed in his own or any former generation; it seemed to arise from a special instinct, aided by something of the nature of genius. The best of the anglers that happened to cope with him were ever the readiest to acknowledge his unapproachable superiority, and not less the modesty with which he bore his triumphs, and the utter unselfishness with which he put his instructions, his example, and his materials, at the service of the brethren. In curling and bowling, in various indoor games of skill or calculation, he was a proficient, having a natural aptitude for them all, and doing with all his might whatever he designed to do. But still it was as an angler that he was most widely known, and most eminent. The sorrow common to all who knew him has a special aggravation to those who companioned with him as an angler the memory of so many merry meetings saddened so many bright scenes, associated with the ideas of rest and cheerfulness, darkened evermore."

AUTHOR'S PREFACE.

Most anglers meet with fair success when the waters are dark coloured; but when the waters are clear they find poor sport. This is mainly due to an erroneous system of fishing, which angling works already published have done little to remove, and which, though its effects were not so observable fifty years ago, when drainage was less extensively in operation, and when the streams continued large and discoloured for some time, is not at all adapted for the small clear waters of the present day. It is with the view of showing how almost, if not quite, as good sport may be had in clear water as in coloured, that we have undertaken to add another to the numerous volumes already existing upon this very popular amusement. It is almost unnecessary to add, that as it is more difficult to deceive trout in clear water than in coloured, the method of angling which succeeds best in the one case will also succeed best in the other.

For more than fifteen years we have pursued angling with the greatest assiduity; and during that period have obtained information from a number of excellent amateur anglers (among whom we may mention the Secretary of the late St. Ronan's Angling Club), to all of whom we take this opportunity of expressing our thanks. We have also fished with, and watched while fishing, almost all the best professional anglers of the day, including the celebrated James Baillie, considered by all who knew him the ablest fly-fisher in Scotland, and from whom we have received some valuable information upon that branch of the art; and it must be admitted that there are few anglers like those whose ingenuity and perseverance are stimulated by necessity. The information received from these we have thoroughly tested before admitting it into the following pages, and we may safely say that we have gained more from half-an-hour's conversation with such, than from all the books we ever read upon the subject, and their number is not small; most works upon angling being rather amusing than instructive. The angler will not find this the case in the following volume: if he finds nothing instructive, he will certainly find nothing amusing; and we found our claims to the attention of the angling community solely upon the ground of the information we have to convey, which we have endeavoured to make as distinct as possible; and as this treatise is only intended for anglers, we expect that the style and composition will not be very severely criticised.

EDINBURGH, *January* 1857.

CONTENTS.

	PAGE
INTRODUCTION TO NEW EDITION	XXXI

By W. EARL HODGSON.

CHAPTER 1.
INTRODUCTORY.

Enthusiasm of Anglers—Attractions of Angling—Trout the Fish most sought after—Excuses of Anglers—Defective Memory of Anglers 1

CHAPTER II.
FRESH-WATER TROUT.

Senses of Trout—Slow-running Streams—Various Productiveness of Streams—Voracity of the Trout—Effects of Drainage—Tweed—The Harry-Water Net—Increase of Anglers—Effects of much Fishing 13

CHAPTER III.
ANGLER'S EQUIPMENT.

Fishing - boots—Fishing - rods—Different Woods used in Rod-making—Joining of the Rod—Reels—Gut—Methods of staining Gut—Hooks—Landing or Minnow Nets 33

CHAPTER IV.

ARTIFICIAL FLY-FISHING.

Pre-eminence of Fly—fishing—Value of the Artificial Fly—Difficulty of Fly-fishing—Errors of Fly-fishers—Advantages of Fishing up Stream—Ordinary method of Fly-fishing—Size or Colour of Water—Fishing up not suitable for Salmon—Stupidity of Anglers 55

CHAPTER V.

FLIES, FLY-DRESSING, ETC.

Odd Notions respecting Flies—The May-fly of England—Trout's Ideas of Artificial Flies—Spider-flies—Feathers for making Spiders— The most killing Flies—Method of dressing a Spider—Method of dressing a Fly—Difficulty of dressing Flies neatly—Formation of the Fly-cast—The Fly-rod — Casting-powers of Rods 76

CHAPTER VI.

ON TROUTING WITH THE FLY.

Disadvantages of a long Line—Striking the Trout —How to fish Pools, Streams, etc.—Repeated Casting necessary—Sizes of Fly—General Rules—"Time of the Take"—May as a Fly-fishing Month—Flies for May—Night-fishing —Maggots as an addition to Fly—Advice to Beginners 104

CHAPTER VII.

ON ANGLING WITH THE WORM.

PAGE

Tackle necessary—Size of Hook—Experiments upon Hooks—Sinkers—Different kinds of Worms—Size of Worm—Necessity of fishing up Stream—Necessity of keeping little Line in Water—Method of fishing Streams—Best time of Day—Places where to Fish—Effect of East Wind—Angling in Flooded Waters—Worm-fishing in Hill-burns 134

CHAPTER VIII.

MAY-FLY FISHING.

Natural History of the May-fly—Canister for holding Flies—Method of using the Creeper—Method of using the May-fly 163

CHAPTER IX.

MINNOW AND PARR-TAIL FISHING.

Methods of capturing Minnows—Size of Minnow—Drag-hooks—Method of Baiting the Minnow—Most favourable Condition of Water—Places where to Fish—Best Weather for using the Minnow—Method of Baiting the Parr-tail 173

CHAPTER X.

LOCH-FISHING.

PAGE

Loch-trout—Loch-flies—Size of Flies—Too thick Gut generally used—How to fish a Loch—Fishing in a Calm—Loch Leven Trout—Trolling—Tackle—Best Method of Trolling—Worm-fishing in Lochs 192

CHAPTER XI.

APPLICATION.

Salmon-roe—Protection of Parr—General Advices—Best means of filling a Basket in May—End of the Angling Season 214

INDEX 227

INTRODUCTION.

MESSRS. ADAM AND CHARLES BLACK believe that a new edition of "The Practical Angler; or, The Art of Trout-Fishing, More Particularly Applied to Clear Water," would find a welcome. All who have read the work, which was first published about fifty years ago, will share this feeling. Most of these will know that serviceable books of instruction in the art of Angling are remarkably rare. Of the many persons who have written on the sport, a few only have had the gift of teaching. Perhaps this is because the subject presents a strong temptation to the lyrical instincts, which are apt to stray into aimlessness; perhaps it is because, taking Isaac Walton as their exemplar, not a few writers on Angling have, as teachers, been hampered by a desire to excel in form and style. Mr. Stewart's essay is an outstanding exception. It is a masterly accomplishment of a difficult task undertaken with engaging modesty. Both the sportsman and the critic of literature will find it admirable. Mr.

Stewart knew all that was known about trout and the methods of catching them; and, like "A Son of the Marshes" in later years, he was singularly well endowed with the knack of presenting his knowledge on the printed page. Throughout the volume there are sentences that could be analysed opprobriously by any grave boy fresh from school; but what of that? Mr. Pinkerton, in "The Wrecker," an amiable youth with a passion for culture, was inclined to sniff at a certain newspaper report of a mishap at sea; and Mr. Loudon Dodd, his mentor, through whom spake Mr. Robert Louis Stevenson, assured him that the report was "a good, honest, plain piece of work," telling the story clearly. So is "The Practical Angler." It stands in relation to literature as pleasantly as a well-thrown fly-line to the sport itself. It has that peculiar and complete sincerity, the secret of which seems neither communicable not to be defined, which marks all works that live beyond their day and generation.

On reading "The Practical Angler" we perceive cause for being fairly well pleased with the state of the trout-streams. Mr. Stewart, when he fished and wrote, was obviously disposed to think that the sport was destined to decline. He lamented the agricultural drainage, which "was less extensively in operation" fifty years before. "So long as drainage *was confined to the rivers' banks, its effects were not so observable; but now that it has extended to the recesses of the mountains, whence most of our rivers receive nine-tenths of their water, and every hill, glen, and moor is drained, it tells severely upon the streams and their inhabitants. The water, which used to find its way to the rivers gradually, keeping them large and full for a considerable time, is now conducted to them soon after the rain falls, and runs off in a day or two, leaving them clear and dwindled till the next flood." One can understand Mr. Stewart's misgiving. It seemed certain that the new drainage would have worse results than leaving the streams for long periods smaller than Nature designed. "It is supposed that the heavy floods we now have shift the gravel and carry off a large quantity of the spawn of the trout, and also of the eggs of the aquatic insects. When the waters are very small, the eggs of the aquatic insects are left dry, and their vitality destroyed, so that the number of insects upon which trout feed is materially lessened, and at the same time the number and size of trout, which depend in a great measure upon the quantity of food." The prospect was undoubtedly depressing; but, as it has not been quite fulfilled in half a century, anglers may take heart of hope.*

What Mr. Stewart said about the great floods, and

the long spells of too little water, was, and still is, true; yet, as far as can be gathered from the available data, which are vague, the trout in most of the streams are flourishing almost as well as they ever were. It is admitted that the May-fly, a very nourishing food, has disappeared from many waters, and perhaps other insects less noticeable have gone; which may justify and account for the statements, to be heard from old anglers in many parts, that the trout have fallen off in size. We must, however, make allowance for the tendency to glorify the old days and depreciate the current ones. All the things first seen in youth, even the hills about one's native place, are larger in retrospect than in reality. Besides, the science of fish-culture is new and quickly progressive. Aquatic insects as well as trout are being systematically studied. Wherever the Mayflies once fluttered we may see them again ere long. If the eggs do not survive in the main streams, perhaps they may thrive near the mouths of the tributaries. If so, they may spread when given a chance anew. It is not inconceivable that the Mayfly might adapt itself to the unstable conditions of the streams. Perhaps, indeed, these were not the main causes of its disappearance here and there. It is possible that the main cause was pollution from town-drainage, distilleries, and such factories as starch-mills. Slime on the bed of

INTRODUCTION

a river would prevent the eggs of the insects from coming to life. Since "The Practical Angler" was first published, Parliament has passed measures against pollution, and nearly everywhere there is a growing public opinion in favour of enforcing the Acts.

Mr. Stewart's discourse on Rods is not now to be taken literally. First-class rods to-day are other and better than those with which Mr. Stewart filled his capacious creel. The art of building with split-cane has produced a new weapon. It has itself resulted in a rod of excellent type, originally American, and it has led to successful refinement in rods of greenheart or other wood. Mr. Stewart's favourite rod, the parts of which were put together by splicing, seems to have weighed fourteen ounces; with brass joints, he says, it would have weighed "about a pound and a half, nearly double the weight, which tells fearfully upon the angler's arm in fly-fishing;" and the difficulties with which the makers of fifty years ago had to contend may be understood from the remark about "two feet extra length in a rod entailing at least a half more weight." Nowadays rod-making is a highly specialised craft. The ferrules are tempered to prevent their involving patches of unbending stiff-ness. They add so little to the weight that a twelve-foot rod, strong enough to manage the heaviest trout, need not be more than ten ounces.

There are, indeed, rods much lighter. One can now have a nine-foot four-ounce wand that is not to be deemed a toy. "The rod for fly-fishing from a boat," says Mr. Stewart in Chapter X., "need not be longer than thirteen or fourteen feet, as that is long enough to keep the angler out of sight, and a very long rod is cumbrous to manage. In angling from the bank, a rod two feet longer might be advisable, in order to reach the places where the trout lie." At this rate a trout-rod built after the specification of Mr. Stewart would have all the dimensions of a modern salmon one! The explanation lies mainly in the primitive methods according to which the rod-makers of his time managed their material. If the wood were filed thin, it ceased to have strength enough. At least, the makers thought so. Since then the "steel centre" for built cane, and other devices for strengthening and stiffening, have been invented, and simultaneously anglers have gradually discovered that the old rods were unnecessarily long. Mr. Stewart's preference of thirteen or fourteen feet as the length of a rod for lake-fishing must have been based upon a misconception. Seated in a boat an angler is considerably lower, in relation to the surface of the water, than he is on the bank of a stream; and, as many of the fish may be looking not towards the boat but away from it, he is therefore rather less likely to be seen by the fish when on a lake than he is when by the side of a river. Then, the lighter the rod the more quickly does the turn of the wrist in striking tell, and the less is the danger of a breakage with a heavy fish. Indeed, there seems reason for believing that the lightest of rods is often the best-suited to lake-fishing. There is usually a breeze to help in getting the flies away. On the other hand, a four-ounce rod will not bring a large trout to the landing-net so quickly as a heavier one will, and this must be a consideration when big fish are rising. What, then, it may be asked, are the dimensions of the ideal rod? The answer is that the ideal is not embodied in any single type. To be equipped against all emergencies, the angler must have more than one rod. Length and weight are to be determined less by the size of the fish than by the width of the stream. A very light nine-foot rod will not be too frail for a very heavy fish; but, especially in an unfavourable wind, it will not make a very long cast. Some of the rivers that Mr. Stewart frequented, such as the Tweed, call for a rod of twelve feet and equivalent weight, or even a little longer and weightier; but very many trout-streams are so much less broad that a rod so large would be out of place on them. The essential principle is that a light rod strikes more quickly, more delicately, and more effectively than one less light. For any particular stream, then, the most suitable rod is the lightest that will throw a fly, without undue strain, to any part of the water, in the ordinary course, where a trout may be rising or lurking. I myself find that three rods are equal to all the opportunities of a holiday on well-varied waters. One of them, nine feet long, weighs four ounces and a half; another, eleven feet, weighs eight ounces; the third is twelve feet, and weighs twelve ounces.

Other passages in "The Practical Angler" tempt to comment. There is an account, for example, of the "drag" that Mr. Stewart attached to his spinning-tackle. The drag was "to catch by the outside of the body those trout which bite shy or miss the minnow." Happily, there having been enactments which may be construed as rendering it unlawful, that device need not be discussed. Then, as to the qualities of light, the colour of water, and the eyesight of trout, our author acted and advised upon questionable assumptions. "Highland lochs," we read, "are generally of a dark colour, which helps to disguise the angler's tackle." That is an illusion. To anyone walking by the side of a Highland loch, or even afloat on parts so deep that the bottom is invisible, the water does at times seem dark; but in truth, excepting in extreme flood, it is always crystal-clear from the trout's point of view, much clearer, as a rule, than that of a stream. I mention this because Mr. Stewart's error has a strange persistence. It is repeated in book after book about Angling. The aspect presented by water to the human eye is often deceptive. Does not even a chalk-stream seem clouded in a pool with a muddy bottom? It does; yet the same water flowing over sand or gravel, just afterwards, is seen to be pellucid.

All matters such as these, however, are properly to be left to the consideration of the reader. He that has the honour of being asked to write an Introduction to a work so well reputed as "The Practical Angler" should not set to himself the task of the reviewer.

It remains to comply with the Publishers' wish that the flies used by Mr. Stewart should be presented in colour. I will make a list of the lures, specifying the dressings; send it to Mr. P. D. Malloch, Perth, asking him to make flies according to the written patterns; and have plates of the images inset just before the opening chapter. I have thought of Mr. Malloch because, besides being familiar with all the waters in which Mr. Stewart fished, he is a learned naturalist and one of the most expert of anglers. Mr. Stewart was somewhat empirical as regards both the textures and the sizes of his lures. He did not think it necessary that an artificial fly should invariably resemble a real one, and was disposed to flout the idea that imitations of all the real flies were desirable. Lures without wings, or with spent wings, he spoke about as "spiders." Now known as "spinners," they are imitations of flies that have been laying eggs and have had their wings tattered in passing through the water. Mr. Stewart used large flies when the water was rough or discoloured, and less large when it was normal or small. I will ask Mr. Malloch to show the loch flies in two sizes, and, as regards those for streams, to choose what are now the standard sizes while adopting the textures with exactitude. That will be fair to Mr. Stewart, and helpful to readers of the book.

W. EARL HODGSON.

Spring, 1905.

A BOOK OF FLIES

for

LOCH AND STREAM

as used by

MR. STEWART

Fly Plate Notes - 2009

The Practical Angler, first published in 1857, was reprinted many times before the appearance of the first illustrated edition in 1905. The colour plates in the 1905 and subsequent editions were of "A book of flies for loch and stream as used by Mr. Stewart, reproduced in facsimile". These took the form of colour photographs of leaves from a fly-wallet holding flies especially tied for that edition by P.D. Malloch of Perth.

The present publisher took the view that Malloch's flies, tied almost fifty years after Stewart was writing, were not always tied exactly to Stewart's methods, and were not necessarily more authentic than flies that we might tie today. Accordingly, Terry Griffiths was commissioned to reproduce and photograph a new set of flies, being as faithful to Malloch's plates as possible, but closely following Stewart's methods.

Only natural fly-tying materials were used, the hooks are blind Dublin Bend of the period, and the gut attachment is also the genuine article. The only substitute used is with the Dotterel Spider - where a feather from the underside of a jack starling wing, as suggested by Mr. Stewart, is used instead of the long-protected dotterel.

The choice of flies for the original plates well illustrates the varied skills of the fly-tyer, particularly making/building/tying rolled, slip and matched-pair wings, a fact not fully understood by Terry until the work was well under way.

LOCH FLIES (Rolled Wings).

1. *Jay & Blue*
2. *Jay & Yellow*
3. *Jay & Purple*
4. *Woodcock & Red*
5. *Woodcock & Brown*
6. *Woodcock & Orange*

STREAM FLIES

7. *Blaewing & Hare's Ear*
8. *Golden Plover Spider*
9. *Woodcock & Yellow*

STREAM FLIES (Nos. 7, 8, 9, Rolled Wings).

1. *Grouse Spider* 2. *Dotterel Spider* 3. *Partridge Spider*
4. *Dark Starling Spider* 5. *Black Spider* 6. *Red Spider*
7. *Corncrake & Orange* 8. *Starling & Brown* 9. *Woodcock & Red*

MAY FLIES

1. Green Drake

2. Grey Drake

3. Spent Gnat

LOCH FLIES (Nos. 4, 5, 6, 7, 8, 9, Rolled Wings)

1. Heckham & Yellow
2. Heckham & Green
3. Heckham & Red
4. Jay & Blue
5. Jay & Yellow
6. Jay & Purple
7. Woodcock & Red
8. Woodcock & Brown
9. Woodcock & Orange

LOCH FLIES (Large).

1. Teal & Yellow
2. Teal & Green
3. Teal & Red
4. Grouse & Yellow
5. Grouse & Orange
6. Grouse & Green
7. Mallard & Green
8. Mallard & Red
9. Mallard & Yellow

THE PRACTICAL ANGLER.

CHAPTER I.

INTRODUCTORY.

ANGLERS, unlike excisemen, have no ground of complaint against the definition given of their occupation in Johnson's Dictionary. Angling, the world is there informed, is "the art of fishing with a rod." This may be imperfect—may need a little filling up (the task, indeed, which we propose to ourselves)—but it is perfectly fair and unprejudiced. Not so, however, another definition, dropped from the lips of the same great authority in private, and which has ever since passed from mouth to mouth with a sneer. "Angling," said Dr. Johnson, "means a rod with a fly at one end and a fool at the other." Nothing has rankled so deeply in the angling mind as this *obiter dictum* of the Mitre. It came from one, however,

INTRODUCTORY.

who knew nothing whatever about the pursuit at which he threw his sarcasm, who, short-sighted and hypochondriacal, probably could not have enjoyed it had he tried, and who (the fact is sufficient for us) openly proclaimed his preference for the tumult of Fleet Street to the finest rural scene in England. Still we are bound to confess, that the British public is to a considerable extent divided as to which definition is the more correct. There are few amusements which the uninitiated look upon as so utterly stupid; and an angler seems generally regarded as at best a simpleton, whose only merit, if he succeeds, is that of unlimited patience, and whose want of success—should he not succeed—is only attributable to his want of that virtue, of which people seem to take fully more credit for the want than for the possession. Such impressions can only have originated in very confused ideas of both angling and patience; and though it may suit the unsuccessful to abuse angling as "slow" and monotonous, and to quote Dr. Johnson's famous saying—which, so far as they are concerned, is certainly correct—angling, as we hope to show, is by no means either slow or simple, and requires just the same qualifications as are required for success in any other pursuit—viz., energy and skill, and those in no small degree.

If, however, on the one hand, angling is looked upon with little favour by an unenlightened multitude, on the other hand, there is no amusement to which those who practise it become so much attached. Nor do we think that anglers generally can fairly be accused either of stupidity, or, let us say, patience. They have certainly in their ranks a larger proportion of men of literature and science than can be found among the followers of any other field sport; and for the comfort of those who have not the much-despised gift of patience, we could point to a number of celebrated anglers, who are by no means celebrated as possessing this virtue, while numbers of the most patient followers of Izaak Walton are very far from having rivalled his success. Angling, when once embarked in by any person possessed of a reasonable amount of soul and brains, becomes a passion, and like other passions will grow and feed upon the smallest possible amount of encouragement. Fish or no fish, whenever opportunity offers, the angler may be found at the water-side. If this only went on in fine weather, people could understand it, but now-a-days, even in summer, the weather is not always fine; and when a man is seen standing in the water for hours in a torrent of rain, with benumbed hands and an empty basket, doubts of the individual's sanity naturally suggest themselves, mixed with feelings of pity for the terrible consequences in the way of colds, rheumatism, &c., which it is supposed must inevitably follow, but which don't. We have it from high medical authority, that rheumatism is more engendered by hot rooms and fires than by exposure, and as for the comfort of the thing, that is according to taste. It is surely better to have fresh air and exercise, even in wet, than to be spending the whole day in some country inn, yawning over some second-rate novel for the third time, the amusement agreeably diversified by staring out of the window at the interminable rain, by poking a peat-fire, and possibly by indulging in a superfluity of that institution of the country, pale ale.

> "Though sluggards deem it but an idle chase,
> And marvel men should quit their easy chair,
> The toilsome way and long long league to trace;
> Oh! there is sweetness in the mountain air,
> And life that bloated ease can never hope to share."

That angling is good for exercise is certain. That it is also good for amusement is equally certain; but the pleasure derived from the catching of fish, like that derived from other field sports, is more easily felt than described. There can be no doubt, that by the great majority of people an amusement is valued in proportion as it affords room for the exercise of skill—there is more merit, and therefore more pleasure, in excelling in what is difficult—and though we may astonish some of our readers, we assert, and shall endeavour to prove, that angling is the most difficult of all field sports. It requires all the manual dexterity that the others do, and brings more into play the qualities of the mind, observation, and the reasoning faculties. In shooting and hunting, the dogs do the observation and the reasoning part of the business, and the sportsmen the mechanical; but the angler has not only to find out where his fish are but to catch them, and that not by such a "knock-me-down" method as is practised upon some unfortunate blackcock or unwary hare, but by an art of deception. The angler's wits, in fact, are brought into direct competition with those of the fish, which very often, judging from the result, prove the better of the two.

Besides the mere pleasure of fishing, however, angling has more varied attractions than almost any other amusement. To the lover of nature no sport affords so much pleasure. The grandest and most picturesque scenes in nature are to be found on the banks of rivers and lakes. The angler, therefore, enjoys the finest scenery the country offers; and, whereas other sportsmen are limited to particular places and seasons. he can follow his vocation alike on lowland stream or highland loch, and during the whole six months in which the country is most inviting. From April, with her budding trees and singing birds, to May and June, with their meadows decked with the daisy and the primrose, and breezes scented with the hawthorn and wild thyme, and on to autumn, with her "fields white unto the harvest," he sees all that is beautiful—all that is exhilarating—all that is grand and elevating in this world of ours, which, whatever people may say, is not such a bad world after all, if they would only keep bleachfields and blackguards off the rivers' banks.

With this brief resumé of some of the principal attractions of angling we must content ourselves. We have neither space, inclination, nor ability, to do justice to this branch of the subject. Furthermore, it is unnecessary, as the ground in this respect is already fully occupied; and if any one wishes to have all the joys of angling set forth in genuine old English style, let him read Izaak Walton, "being a discourse on fish and fishing not unworthy the perusal of most anglers." Here may be found a conglomeration of fertile meadows, crystal brooks, meandering streams, milk-maids' songs, and moral reflections, which must prove irresistible; and also, if a man of tender conscience, be able to satisfy himself that angling is not a cruel amusement, though it must be admitted that some of Izaak's injunctions, such as putting a hook "through a frog tenderly, as though you loved him,"—seeing that the said tenderness is to be evinced, not for the sake of saving the frog's feelings, but of prolonging its wretched life—do savour a little of harshness, and seem to justify Lord Byron's lines :—

"The quaint old cruel coxcomb in his gullet
Should have a hook, and a small trout to pull it."

Never having had any scruples of this sort ourselves, we have not studied the subject, and therefore leave the defence of it to Walton and a celebrated Doctor of Divinity who has taken it in hand; but if any one has any scruples, or thinks angling slow and stupid, or has any other objections, let him keep clear of it, by all means. There are plenty of anglers already, and every year adds to the list a number who are not to be deterred either by the sneers of this world, or by terror of the punishment, which, the poet thinks, should be reserved for the master, and we suppose for all his followers, in the next; and our purpose is not to make more anglers, but to make successful anglers of those unsuccessful at present.

Some fish afford more sport in their capture than others; but for whatever kind necessity may compel the angler to fish, its capture will always afford him amusement, provided he has not been accustomed to anything superior. The juvenile cockney who bobs for gudgeon and eels in the dubs and ditches in the neighbourhood of London, and whom a trout of a pound weight would scare out of a year's growth, plies his lure as unremittingly as the sportsman who captures the monarch of the streams in some noble river, such as Tweed or Tay.

Of all the inhabitants of the fresh water, no fish is looked upon with such favour by the angler, and none affords him such varied and continuous sport, as the common fresh-water trout. This is owing to its being the most difficult to capture of all the finny tribe, not excepting the salmon itself, to the sport it affords when hooked—the trout being stronger than any fish of its size—and to its fine edible qualities.

In some parts of England trout have almost disappeared, and the angler has been compelled to have recourse to meaner fare; but in Scotland trout are more plentiful than any other fish, and trout-fishing is within the reach of all. The difficulty is not to name a river where good sport may be had, but to name a river where good sport may not be had, if properly gone about. Railway travelling has afforded the angler great facilities for the pursuit of his vocation. One, or at most two hours' ride will convey all lovers of sport in any large town in Scotland, and in most of those in England, to streams where there are plenty of trout; and, to do them justice, they avail themselves of it to the utmost. On a holiday the banks of any stream in the neighbourhood are thickly studded with anglers, a few of whom meet with good sport, but the greater number, having demolished their sandwiches and emptied their flasks, return with their baskets, and occasionally their heads, lighter than when they left home. Happily, however, and it is certainly a strong argument in favour of the attractions of angling, they are not a whit discouraged; but, on the contrary, eager to return first opportunity, and have always a good excuse for their want of success. We never yet met a bad angler that had not a good excuse; sometimes it is clear water, sometimes a bright day, sometimes thunder in the air, very often too many white clouds; and failing all these, there still remains the great excuse which is equally applicable to all states of weather and water, that somehow or other the trout would not take—all of which we dismiss upon the ground that they should take the trout. Anglers have also an extraordinary knack of raising, hooking, and playing, but losing large trout. The trout once escaped, there is ample scope for the imagination to conjecture its probable size.

We have never heard of any phrenologist having made the discovery that persons addicted to angling lack or lose the faculty of correctly distinguishing the essential properties of all matter—number, size, and ponderosity. It is certain, however, that in relation to fish they frequently show a lamentable deficiency in this power. Or, to take the harsher view that we fear finds too much favour with a censorious world, they are in too many cases guilty of habitual and most intolerable exaggerations, not to use a stronger word. We think it a duty on the part of all sober-minded and truthful anglers, to set their faces against this vice, and to expose its "hideous mien" on all occasions. It has brought a stigma on our fraternity; it has been the cause of many a day's disappointment to believing listeners; and it has a tendency to propagate itself, for an honestly disposed angler is often through it himself driven to desert the ways of truth, in order that his "take" may not sink into utter insignificance beside that of a more boastful but less veracious companion. Returning recently from a day's fishing, which had been cut short by a violent thunderstorm, we encountered at the railway station a well-known angler, and waited till the appointed time, well pleased to listen to his pleasant stories about angling, holding a foremost place amongst which were tales of his having detected the frauds and impostures of bragging brethren. Of his own spoiled sport that day he remarked that he had only caught four trouts, but that they weighed half-a-pound each. The statement naturally excited surprise and suspicion. Such an "average" in that particular stream was unusual on any day; and on this occasion, as no trout of that size had come our way, or that of the friends who were with us, we had arrived at the conclusion that the "good ones" were sulking, as they will sometimes do. In the railway carriage the man of half-pounders stuck to his statement, but refused to lead evidence by showing his fish. Aided by our friends, however, we succeeded in temporarily poinding his pannier, and dived into its depths. There, amidst boots, stockings, empty flasks, and sandwich papers, we discovered the concealed trouts. Troutkins, rather—not trouts! half-pounders!—the whole four together would scarcely have weighed half-a-pound. Whether it was a too lively imagination that had caused the discrepancy between the ideal trouts of the platform and the real trouts of the basket, we care not to inquire; but we wonder if the same angler will ever again multiply the weight of his take by four, or by any other figure, or whether, made wise by experience, and by this crushing exposure, he will carefully take note of the size of his fish before consigning them to his basket, and not trust to a hasty glance to impress a memory which, let us charitably suppose, may be defective. At all events, people who do not put a padlock on their baskets ought to put one on their mouths.

Some anglers have also a habit of characterising large takes as butchery; the point where sport stops and butchery commences lying about the individual's greatest take. We cannot see the justice of an opinion that considers the capture of a certain number of trout sport, and of twice that number—taken by the same means—butchery. If the sport of angling lies in the capture of fish, it seems evident that the more fish the better sport; and it is our intention to treat of the different branches of angling solely with the view of showing how the greatest weight of trout can be captured in a given time. There are not many days from May till October, in which an angler, thoroughly versed in all the mysteries of the craft, should not kill at least twelve pounds weight of trout in any county in the south of Scotland, not

INTRODUCTORY.

excepting Edinburghshire itself.* And to describe the way in which this may be done is our object in this small volume.

* [This statement might be held as pretty nearly correct at the time Mr. Stewart wrote it—at least, taking into account his then ideas and habits as to "a day," which a jealous gamekeeper, whom he had always utterly beaten, described as "twenty-four hours of creeping and crawling." In point of fact, Mr. Stewart, during summer, liked to be on the water soon after sunrise, and he continued with little intermission till towards four in the afternoon. In his later years he had not strength for work so severe, but still would not fail to begin by seven o'clock. Even those possessing the requisite strength, and a good share of Mr. Stewart's unequalled skill, would now fail to procure 12 lbs. on "many days" "in any county in the south of Scotland," so rapid has been the increase of pollutions and drainage, and of anglers. Subsequent to the first edition of his work, Mr. Stewart had seen cause to reduce his figures, although he allowed his original statement to stand in the body of the work (see p. 153); and it is known that before his death he confessed to a necessity still further to lower his estimate.]

CHAPTER II.

FRESH-WATER TROUT.

THE *Salmo fario*, or common trout, is indigenous to almost every river, burn, and loch in Scotland. When in good condition no tenant of the stream surpasses it in beauty of appearance. The head is small and well-shaped, the back finely curved, and the sides are thickly studded with starlike spots of a variety of colours, from bright red to dark brown. It is singular that it is a most unusual occurrence to find two trouts spotted exactly alike, there being generally some difference, however slight. Why it is so is beyond elucidation—probably for the same reason that no two human beings are the same in form and face.

The trout of one stream can sometimes be distinguished from those of another; but this is more by the complexion and shape, than by any arrangement of the spots; and these are well known to be entirely the result of feeding, and of the distinctive characteristics of each stream. Trout taken from a dark mossy water are dark and ill-coloured, while those taken from a clear stream are of a corresponding colour. Trout caught under a bank, in the shade of a bush, or in a part of the river where the bottom is dark, are of a darker colour than those caught in the lighter and more open parts; their complexion thus changing according to the colour of the water they inhabit, the colour of the ground over which they move, and the degree of light.

It is not our province to enter into the natural history of the trout, as what anglers wish to know is how to capture them, and we shall therefore consider trout in a purely angling point of view.

With regard to the much-vexed question of whether trout hear or not, naturalists say that they have ears, but we think that these organs are rather intended by nature to convey any agitation in the water, to which they are keenly alive, than external noise. This much seems evident, that no noise out of the water can be heard by a trout in it. Guns have been fired not many yards from trout, but they exhibited no symptoms of alarm, which they would certainly have done had they heard; and, though some English works upon angling caution the angler against speaking loud at the water-side for fear of alarming the fish, this much is certain, that neither by speaking, nor any other noise the angler can make, is there the least danger of alarming them. They have frequently been caught below a railway bridge at the very time a train was passing overhead.

Those who object to fishing on the ground of its cruelty have got into nice disquisitions upon the subject of trouts' feelings. Having already referred our readers to Izaak Walton and a learned Doctor of Divinity for the solution of this difficulty, we need not do more than remark that their feelings do not seem to be by any means acute. They have frequently been caught with flies in their mouths which had been left there by some angler a few hours previous. The trout, as Professor Wilson observed, having gone off, "with a fly in one cheek and his tongue in the other." A friend of ours met with a remarkable instance of this want of feeling when angling in the Whitadder with worm. He had just made his first cast when a trout went off with the whole apparatus of hook and casting-line. Without moving from where he stood, in the middle of the water, he put on another, and first cast with it caught the trout with the previous casting-line hanging from its mouth, and the hook firmly fixed in it. The vagaries which they exhibit when hooked are usually attributed to pain, but more probably arise from a mixed feeling of surprise and just indignation at having their powers of locomotion suddenly curtailed.

Of all the senses trout possess, that of sight is the most perfect, and is the one which most affects the angler in pursuit of his vocation. Naturalists say that the appearance and structure of the eye do not lead to the conclusion that their sight is very acute; but the angler has every reason to believe otherwise. They can detect the smallest fly even in running water; and at night, when it is so dark that the angler cannot see his flies, or even his rod, trout will see and seize a midge-fly, which certainly argues the possession of extraordinary powers of vision. Their eyes are situated in the front of their head, and looking sideways, so that they not only see in front, but also on both sides of them, and even a little behind.

The growth, size, and edible qualities of trout entirely depend upon the quality and quantity of their food, and these, of course, depend upon the nature of the water they inhabit. The largest and finest trout are usually found in lochs; these yielding more and better food than rivers. The redness in the flesh, which some trout have, is entirely the result of feeding, and is a very good index to their edible qualities. It is quite a common occurrence to capture red and white-fleshed trout in the same loch or river; the red-fleshed ones being merely better fed specimens of the same kind.

Of rivers, those which flow slowly, and are more like canals than rivers, always produce the best trout. Of this description are most of the English streams; and though trout in some of them are now very scarce, they are occasionally caught of large size; indeed, in point of size, shape, and edible qualities, they bear away the palm from any that can be found in our Scottish streams. Among our own streams of this kind are the Eden and the Leven in Fifeshire, the Blackadder and the Leet in Berwickshire, the lower parts of the Clyde in Lanarkshire, and Biggar Water in Peeblesshire. All these streams run very slowly; in some of them there are miles where it is difficult to tell at first sight which way the water is flowing. They all contain large, well-shaped, and in general red-fleshed trout, owing to the superior feeding which such streams, running over a bottom of mud or marl, possess, and also to the circumstance that they are generally not numerous. This last fact is due to a number of causes. Deep, slow-running streams are not favourable for spawning, trout requiring briskly-running, shallow water for that purpose. They are also ill provided with stones and gravel, where the young fry may shelter themselves from their rapacious relatives, and from pike, which generally abound in such places, and commit sad havoc. It is observed that wherever these fresh-water tyrants are found, the trout attain large size, those that escape getting double the quantity of food they would under ordinary circumstances. It seems as if the feeding of a river could only support a certain weight of trout, so that where they are very numerous they are not large, and *vice versâ*. Hence proprietors of ponds sometimes drag them with a net, and take out the small fish to improve the size of the remainder.

Of the opposite class from those just mentioned are very rapid and hard-bottomed streams. Of this kind are most Highland streams, a few in the hilly parts of the Lowlands, and numerous hill-burns. The rapidity with which their waters run, and the smoothness and solidity of their channels, prevent any accumulations taking place which could yield sustenance to the trout, which, in the very height of the season, are poor and soft, and weigh miserably in proportion to their length.

Between the slow-running streams on the one hand, and the very rapid on the other, there is a wide range, comprising all degrees of swiftness; and every angler may get a river in which the variation of stream and pool will be exactly suited to his taste. Like the streams, the trout are of a medium quality, sometimes red in the flesh and sometimes white—depending on the quality and quantity of food they obtain. Of this description are Tweed and its tributaries with few exceptions, most of the streams in the south of Scotland, and a few in the Highlands. In Tweed, trout are occasionally caught six and seven pounds in weight; and we have heard of one being taken from this river of the great weight of twelve pounds, which

SIZE OF TROUT, ETC.

is the largest river trout we have heard of being caught in Scotland; but they are not of such fine quality as those taken from our smaller streams.

We have mentioned the size of trout as almost entirely depending upon the quantity of their food, without reference to age; indeed this has but little to do with the question, and there being no mark by which their age may be known, any opinion upon this point must be in a great measure conjectured, and cannot well be tested by experiment, as trout will hardly increase in size at all unless free to seek their food and range the water as they please. We believe that a ten-year-old trout may not weigh half-a-pound, or may weigh six pounds, according to the quality and quantity of its food.

The number of trout a river produces depends upon a variety of natural causes, the principal of which is the spawning accommodation. Rivers in which there are plenty of smooth gravelly stretches, and which receive numerous small tributaries, generally produce numbers of trout—shallow water and a gravelly bottom being necessary for the deposit of the spawn. If a river is scantily furnished with spawning accommodation and also with food, the trout will neither be numerous nor large;—the Spey, the Dee, the Esk (Dumfriesshire), and most Highland streams, are examples of this. If the spawning accommodation is deficient and the feeding good, the trout are large, as in most slow-running streams. If the spawning accommodation is good and the supply of food limited, the trout are generally numerous but small;—Manor and Quair in Peeblesshire, and some of the tributaries of the Whitadder in Berwickshire, are examples of this, in any of which the angler may easily capture from ten to fifteen dozen of trout any day in summer.

Small rivers produce more trout in proportion to their size than large ones, as a large river has not so much bed in proportion to its volume of water; and it is principally the bed of a river which yields the insects and other food upon which trout live. Rivers where the salmon-fry, or parr, as they are usually called, are very numerous, are rarely such good trouting-streams as those where there are none, the small fish consuming a large proportion of the food of the river. Placing some obstruction at the mouth of a stream in order to prevent the migratory species from ascending it, would improve materially the size of the common trout it contains. Gala and Leader Waters are examples of this. At the mouth of the former there are mill-caulds which salmon cannot get over; near the mouth of the latter a rarely-surmounted waterfall; consequently there are no parr, and the trout are much larger than in any similar tributaries of the Tweed where parr are to be found. A proprietor on the Leader made a well-meant but injudicious attempt to let salmon up; happily, as it has proved, with little success; and we think it is not worth while spoiling the trouting qualifications of such a stream as the Leader, in order to secure a few ill-conditioned salmon in the end of the season. Clean fish will never ascend so small a stream, and it will afford encouragement to some idle vagabonds to poach in winter.

The trout is unquestionably a voracious feeder, and when hungry is not at all particular as to what it satisfies its appetite upon. Flies and aquatic insects of all descriptions, minnows and other small fish, worms, beetles, snails, and frogs are equally victims to its rapacity; nor does it feel any compunctions in devouring the smaller members of its own species. We once, when angling with the minnow in Leader Water, caught a trout of five or six ounces in weight with the tail of a fish protruding about an inch from its mouth, on pulling out which we found it to be a trout in a partially digested state, which, when its neighbour swallowed it, must have weighed at least two ounces. This did not prevent it from rising at the minnow, but its mouth being so full it could not get hold of it, and it was only after repeated rises that it was caught by the outside of the mouth.

All this might lead to the supposition that trout would be easily captured; but this is a great error. Whether it arises from any superior natural endowments, or is merely the result of education, as they are more fished for than any other fish, and may from that cause be more wide-awake; this much is certain, that they are the most wary and difficult to capture of all the inhabitants of the waters, displaying a caution and sagacity in taking their food truly astonishing. They are also the most capricious of all fish, taking greedily one day what they will hardly look at the next. The wariness which trout display varies greatly according to circumstances. A well-fed trout is at all times more wary than a half-starved one, as it can afford to allow a suspicious-looking fly or bait to pass, whereas the other cannot. In rivers much fished, trout, although sometimes numerous, become very shy; seeing artificial flies so often, and being deceived by them, they detect their nature, thus showing that they are to some extent possessed of memory.

The only point relating to trout in an angling point of view, which remains to be considered, is the season when they are in condition. Generally speaking, they are in condition from the middle of April to the middle of September, but this entirely depends upon the nature of the river and season. They are never in condition till they get abundance of insect food. The supply of this keeps pace with the vegetation on the river's banks, and if the season is advanced, trout, in streams which flow through an early district of country, are quite fit for the table by the beginning of April; if the season is backward, they may be fully a month later of coming into condition. In all streams

DECREASE OF TROUT.

trout are in their best condition when the Mayflies are just done, which is generally about the end of June. They continue in condition all July, but subsequently begin to fall off—those that are red fleshed losing their colour, and all kinds becoming pale and soft; and by the end of September or beginning of October are quite full of spawn and hardly worth capturing. It requires very little experience to tell whether or not a trout is in condition; the small head in proportion to the body, and the breadth and thickness of the body itself, at once indicate the well-conditioned fish. All anglers should confine their operations to that period of the year when trout are fit for the table, as it is unsportsman-like in the highest degree to kill fish that are of no use. Such being our opinion, we shall limit the consideration of angling to the months in which trout are in condition.

During the last twenty years a great decrease has taken place in the quantity of trout in our southern streams, and any angler who has been in the habit of frequenting regularly a particular stream during that time must have noticed an almost annual diminution in the number, and still more in the size, of its finny inhabitants. This is an alarming fact, and well worthy the attention of the angling community, as some of the most fruitful causes of this disastrous result might be stopped. Some of them, however, there is no help for, and the most prejudicial of these is the drainage of the land, more particularly of the hill-pastures for sheep. So long as drainage was confined to the river's banks, its effects were not so observable; but now that it has extended to the recesses of the mountains, whence most of our rivers receive nine-tenths of their water, and every hill, glen, and moor is drained, it tells severely upon the streams and their inhabitants. The water, which used to find its way to the rivers gradually, keeping them large and full for a considerable time, is now conducted to them very soon after the rain falls, and runs off in a day or two, leaving them clear and dwindled till the next flood.

Several old residents on Tweedside have assured us, that fifty years ago, when there was a flood, Tweed continued the dark porter colour, so highly prized by anglers, for a week or more, and then ran clear but pretty full. Now the flood is very heavy for the first day or two, and then falls rapidly, in three or four days becoming quite clear, and for weeks scarcely half the size of what it used to be when at its smallest.

It is supposed that the heavy floods we now have shift the gravel, and carry off a large quantity of the spawn of the trout, and also of the eggs of aquatic insects. Then, again, when the waters are very small, the eggs of aquatic insects are left dry. and their vitality destroyed, so that the number of insects upon which trout feed is materially lessened, and at the same time the number and size of trout, which, as has just been stated, depends in a great measure upon the quantity of food. If drainage, for which there is no remedy, has such an injurious effect, there is the more necessity for looking after the causes which might be stopped; and the worst of these are the manufactories, bleachfields, etc., which are so thickly studded along the banks of our southern streams, and which send their dyes and other deleterious refuse straight into the streams, causing sad havoc. When we mentioned this in our first edition, the "Border Advertiser" came down upon us as having fallen into "the vulgar or rather urban error, that manufactories injured the fishing" It would be worse than useless to argue the point with a man living upon the banks of Gala Water. If Gala Water from Galashiels to Tweed, which, to use the words of Mr. Stoddart, "is an unseemly ditch, full of the blackest and most noxious dyes," and which the "Border Advertiser" must see and smell daily, will not convince him, no argument will. Why, the "Man of Ross," who has propounded the rather startling theory that grilse are not young salmon, and whose theory "Blackwood's Magazine" has settled for ever, labours under no such hallucination as our friend the "Advertiser." That manufactories, however, do injure the fishing, all England proves; there, the refuse from them and the drainage of towns are conveyed into the streams, and the result is that salmon are extinct, and trout are fast going. Even in Scotland several streams have suffered severely from these causes, and they are daily increasing. The following graphic, and we fear prophetic, foreshadowing of the fate of Tweed, is taken from the "Quarterly Review" for January 1857, and is written by an angler no less celebrated for wielding the rod than the pen :—

"Look at what the Tweed is now in contrast with what will be its look and smell at that not distant *then*. See her and hers rolling along, beautiful and beautifying, through regions where every ruin is history, and every glen is song—gathering her tributes from a thousand hills—from where sweet Teviot sings, unceasingly, its 'farewell to Cheviot's mountains blue;' where pensive Yarrow winds like a silver chain, amid 'the dowie dens;' where, in the sad and silent 'Forest,'

> 'The wildered Ettrick wanders by,
> Loud murmuring to the careless moon,'

till, grown stately, massive, and brimming, 'Tweed's fair river, broad and deep,' wheeling beneath the donjon keep of Norham and the battlements of Berwick, sinks into the ocean as glittering pure as when she broke away from her native hills. Is all this to vanish, and in its place a pestilential sewer? Is that which spreads health and beauty around to become an eyesore, extending over half the breadth of Scotland? Shall the turrets of Abbotsford be reflected from a monster gutter, all stains and stench? Shall fair Melrose, instead of being 'viewed aright by the pale moonlight,' be nosed in the dark? Forbid it, all the powers of Parliament! If, indeed, that prohibition could not be uttered without destroying or impeding the brisk and cheerful industry which has sprung up among these sweet hills, there might be nothing for it but to sigh and submit. But it would be almost profane to doubt that from so great an evil there must be means of escape—that Hawick may prosper, and yet Tweed be preserved."

If trout alone were concerned, there is little doubt that they would be left to their fate, and come to an ignominious, unhonoured, but not unmourned-for end; but now that valuable property in the salmon-fishings is imperilled, there seems some prospect that the powers of Parliament, which have been so pathetically appealed to, may interfere.

Another of the most fruitful causes of the depopulation of our streams is netting, and it has greatly increased of late years. The rivers are now so exceedingly small during summer, that they afford every facility for the successful practice of this illegal method of catching trout. The net used for this purpose is what is usually called "the harry-water net." Nets of this kind are made so light that they can be carried in the pocket, and so complete in structure, that a whole pool may be almost cleaned of its finny inhabitants at a single haul. Tweed and its tributaries suffer more from netting than any other streams in Scotland, and it is most usually carried on in the neighbourhood of towns or villages, where the poachers can find a ready sale for their trout.

There are three remedies which might be adopted to prevent netting. The first, and undoubtedly the most efficacious of these, is to have the rivers watched; but this is so expensive as to render it quite impracticable. Another way is to drive stakes into the principal pools and streams, which would prevent nets being drawn through. During the last few years this has been tried, and we understand with great success, in some streams in the neighbourhood of Hawick. Gala Water was also staked a few years ago, and an association formed for the protection of the river, called the Gala Angling Association, which every angler who visits that stream should join. It is, however, too soon yet to speak of the effects of this upon Gala, but we have no doubt it will prove highly beneficial. Stakes, however, are liable to this objection, that they interfere with the angler while landing a fish, or when using the worm. The last and most feasible plan is to put large stones in the water, which would have the same effect as the stakes, and would not, like them, interfere with the angler, and would also afford shelter to the fish. The last reason we shall assign for the decrease of trout is the enormous increase of anglers of late years; there are twenty anglers now for one there was fifty years ago. A gentleman who resided on Tweedside about the beginning of the present century says that he and one or two others were the only anglers in a district comprising many miles of water. Then, when a flood came, Tweed remained large for ten days, and was swarming with trout so unwary that they could be caught with tackle and flies which a modern angler would reject as totally useless. Look at the state of the case now. How widely different! Every villager has a rod, and uses it, with more effect too than most amateur anglers; and it is not at all uncommon to be unable of an evening to get a single pool or stream to yourself; and on a favourable day in the month of May, "Tweed's fair river, broad and deep," will be fished by many hundred followers of the gentle craft. Now, as almost all these catch a few trout, and some of them catch large basketsful, it is obvious that this must diminish the number of trout. The present scarcity of trout is forcing itself upon the attention of anglers, and it is sometimes suggested that trout should get a jubilee; but apart from the impossibility of ever carrying such a design into execution, this is unnecessary; if net fishing was entirely stopped, the streams would quickly regain a portion at least of their old fame. The trout taken by the rod in some districts are often few compared with those taken by the net. It is not by the dozen, nor yet by the basketful, that net-fishers count their spoils, but by the hundredweight, and this, of course, must speedily thin the trout in any stream, however prolific it may be.

Fair rod-fishing will never seriously injure a stream. Of this Gala Water affords an excellent illustration. The favourite resort of anglers from Edinburgh, it is, or used to be, fished during the angling season by about thirty anglers daily, and supposing they only average two pounds each, it implies the capture of an immense quantity of trout. It also suffers as much from nets as any tributary of the Tweed, and yet in those parts where nets cannot be successfully wrought trout are still numerous. Nor are they by any means contemptible in size; in this respect they will bear comparison with any of the other tributaries of Tweed open to the public. We once took with the minnow, between Bowland and Stow, twenty trout, the whole we got that day, which weighed fifteen pounds, and we never got such a large average size of trout in any of the other tributaries of the Tweed, or even in Tweed itself.

There are not by any means too many anglers; on the contrary, our Scottish waters would accommodate, if properly distributed, twenty times as many as there now are. Tweed and its tributaries alone would, giving each plenty of water to himself, accommodate several thousands every day during the season.

Much fishing, besides to a certain extent thinning the trout, operates against the angler's killing large takes by making the remaining trout more wary; and it is more from this cause than from the scarcity of trout, that so many anglers return unsuccessful from much-fished streams. The waters also now remain brown-coloured for such a short time that the modern angler is deprived, unless on rare occasions, of even this aid to his art of deception; and the clearness of the water and the increased wariness of the trout are the main causes why the tackle of fifty years ago would be found so faulty now. Fifty years ago it was an easy thing to fill a basket with trout, not so now; then there were ten trout for one there is now—the colour of the water favoured the angler, and the trout were comparatively unsophisticated; now filling a basket with trout, at least in some of our southern streams open to the public, when they are low and clear, is a feat of which any angler may be proud. To do so he must oppose craft to craft, and cunning to cunning, and must study very closely the habits and instincts of the trout. Angling is, in fact, every day becoming more difficult, and consequently better worthy of being followed as a scientific amusement. So far from looking upon the increase of anglers with alarm, it ought to be regarded with satisfaction:

the more trout are fished for, the more wary they become; the more wary they are, the more skill is required on the angler's part; and as the skill an amusement requires constitutes one of its chief attractions, angling is much better sport now than it was fifty years ago.

CHAPTER III.

ANGLER'S EQUIPMENT.

DRESS.—The only advice it is necessary to give the angler on this head is, not to select any very gaudy colours, and to avoid any approach to foppery, as trout have the most thorough contempt for a fop, and will not on any account allow themselves to be handled with kid gloves. Nothing is so completely out of place at the water-side as an individual got up with all the elaboration of one of "Punch's" swells. We often wonder what has tempted such an one to leave off sunning himself in Princes Street to astonish the inhabitants of some distant stream. Seriously speaking, however, gaudy colours are apt to attract the notice of the trout, and are perceived by them at a greater distance. Some anglers may think this is being unnecessarily particular; but on a sunny day, when to escape observation the angler will require to crawl up the river's bank, dress becomes a subject of some importance. Every angler ought to furnish himself with a waterproof coat;

they are now made so light that they can be put in the pocket or strapped to the basket, without the least inconvenience. Some anglers, who, we suppose, must belong to the new school of muscular Christians, allege they never feel comfortable till they get wet; but if, as we suppose, the greater number never feel comfortable when they do, a waterproof coat, a wide-awake hat, and wading-boots, will render them quite independent of the weather.

Wading Boots and Stockings.—Anglers who can stand knee-deep in water, for a whole day during any part of the angling season without any danger of suffering from it, require nothing to wade with but a pair of good stout shoes or boots. If the water is very cold, wearing two pairs of stockings instead of one will add to the angler's comfort. Many anglers, however, particularly those whose mode of life is sedentary, cannot expose themselves to wet with any degree of impunity, so that they must either refrain from wading or wear waterproofs of some description. The ordinary leather boots, such as are generally worn by fishermen, are undoubtedly the most substantial article of the kind to be had. The only objection to them, and it is certainly a serious one, is their great weight; the lightest of them when properly ironed weighing four or five pounds each. To leather wading-boots we prefer waterproof stockings, which are now made light as well as substantial, and may be procured at a very moderate price. These waterproof stockings are intended to be worn over the ordinary worsted ones; some even wear two pairs of stockings below them to keep their feet warm in cold weather. Between the waterproof stockings and the boots, to prevent the latter from cutting the former, another pair of worsted stockings must be put.

Waterproof stockings will last a long time, if, after having been used, they are turned inside out to allow the perspiration which accumulates in the inside to dry off, otherwise it will cause the material to rot. Over them the angler should have a pair of good stout shoes, or boots well-ironed. In all boots or shoes meant for wading this should be attended to, or the angler may slip among the stones, and get an unexpected bath some morning. It will also be found an improvement to bore holes in the soles of them to permit the water to escape, as much water about the feet is disagreeable as well as weighty; and wading gear of any description is quite heavy enough in itself. To keep wading boots and shoes soft, and prevent the leather from cracking, it is necessary that when drying they should be well greased. For this purpose we know nothing better than the grease which curriers use for their leather, and which may be had at any currier's.

Rods.—There is no article for an angler's equipment that affords more room for the exercise of taste in its selection than the rod. Rods may be bought at such a moderate price, and withal so much better than any angler can make them for himself, that it is unnecessary to give any instructions for the mechanical part of rod-making, and we shall merely mention what a good rod should be made of, and the qualities it should possess. The two great requisites in a rod we consider to be stiffness and lightness, two qualities exceedingly difficult to combine. The amount of stiffness should be such that, when casting, the forward motion of the rod may be stopped pretty quickly without any recoil of the point taking place. Most of the rods that are to be had ready made in Edinburgh are useless from their excessive pliability, and from what we have seen of English and Irish rods they are still worse. This is not the fault of the rod-makers, who require to suit the public taste, but the fault of anglers who will have their rods made in that manner. We know of no place where a better rod can be had than in Edinburgh if the angler only says that he wishes it stiff. In casting with a supple rod, after propelling the line forward, and stopping the forward motion of the hand, a recoil of the point takes place, which to a considerable extent interferes with the forward motion of the line.

The advantages of a stiff rod are its great superiority in casting; it will throw a longer and a lighter line, and with greater certainty, to any spot the angler wishes. Its advantages, in these respects, are particularly apparent in a windy day, when it is necessary to cast against the wind, or even sideways to it. With a supple rod, in such circumstances, it is almost impossible to get the line out at all. Another great advantage of a stiff rod is its superiority in striking. In striking, by a quick motion of the wrist, the angler moves the rod; if this is done with a supple rod, the part of it in the hand is moved immediately, but not so the point; the rod yields throughout; and the point, by means of which the line is pulled, may almost be said to remain stationary for a moment after striking, and then moves in a slow uncertain manner; very different from the instantaneous sharp strike of a good stiff rod.

Lightness we consider an essential qualification in a rod; the lighter it is, the angler can cast it the oftener, and use it the longer at a time. This, however, is a matter which the angler should regulate for himself, as a rod that will be too heavy for one will be a mere whip in the hands of another.

The butts of rods are frequently made hollow to contain one or more spare points; and to such as have their points made very thin, this is almost indispensable, as it is by no means uncommon for some anglers to demolish one or two of these flimsy articles in a day. If the butt-piece is to be made hollow, it should be made of ash; the boring of it is a very difficult process, and can only be done by a machine. Saplings are also sometimes used for this purpose, in the centre of which there is generally a considerable quantity of pith, which can easily be scooped out, and the hollow space enlarged. We are by no means partial to hollow butts; they require to be made so thick that they destroy the symmetry of the rod, and they never bend from the hand as a well-made rod should. It is only in Scotland that hollow butts are much used. English anglers object to them as destroying the bend of a rod, and carry a spare point in the handle of their landing-net, which is made hollow for that purpose—in our opinion, a great improvement upon the hollow butts. The necessity for spare points would be avoided, if anglers would get their rods made stronger. A moderately stout rod made of good material, with plenty of rings, will stand much more than could be supposed from its appearance, and even if it should break, it can be temporarily repaired in a very short time. If the butt is not made hollow, fir may be substituted for ash with advantage, as it is much lighter, and quite strong enough.

For the middle pieces of a rod, there is nothing like hickory; it possesses elasticity and strength in a great degree, and if properly taken care of, will stand long and frequent use. Good hickory is the most valuable of all woods to the rod maker.

The tops of rods are made of a great many different kinds of wood—hickory, bamboo, lance, logwood, greenheart, and numerous others. The two

JOINING OF THE ROD.

last mentioned are too brittle and too heavy, pressing severely upon the middle pieces, and causing that excessive pliancy which spoils a rod for all useful purposes. Lance, though not so brittle, is open to the latter objection, and if used at all, should be used very sparingly. Hickory and bamboo, particularly the latter, are best suited for tops, and we think the greater part, if not the whole, should be made of bamboo. The strength of bamboo lies in the skin, and in order to turn this to the best account, rod-makers lay two or three slits together, so as to form a complete skin all round. This is much more troublesome than making it of one piece, but is more durable, and with good usage will never break. Rods are sometimes made entirely of bamboo, but they possess no advantage over those in common use, to compensate for the additional expense—a twelve-foot rod of this material costing £3 or £4. For our own use we are exceedingly partial to rods made entirely of cane, with the exception of the top, which is bamboo. They are stiff, strong, and very light; the only objection to them is, that they are liable to take a bend, unless the angler takes care to straighten the pieces before putting them past.

Great diversity of opinion exists as to how the different pieces of a rod should be put together when intended to be used. Some anglers, ourselves included, prefer the tie system, for the following reasons:—A tied rod is not nearly so liable to break as one with brass joints; the wood of a rod requires to be thinned in order to put the brass on, rendering them liable to give way at the joints—a fact which the experience of all anglers will confirm. A tied rod also bends most equally throughout; and no angler will deny that it is the most agreeable to use. The great objection, however, to brass joints is, that, in order to bear their weight, the rod requires to be made so much thicker throughout. A rod of twelve feet, without brass joints, should weigh about fourteen ounces; with brass joints, it will weigh about a pound and a half, nearly double the weight, which tells fearfully upon the angler's arm in fly-fishing. When the tie system is adopted, the splices should be well waxed, as also the thread with which they are tied, otherwise they will be constantly slipping. This mode of joining is objected to by some, on the ground that there is a good deal of time spent in putting the rod up; but we think much more time will be lost by using a rod with the additional weight necessary to stand brass joints.

If the angler cannot be troubled to tie the pieces of his rod together, joints of some kind are indispensable. The old mode of joining was by screw joints; but they do not last, and the plain slip joint has entirely superseded them, and is undoubtedly the most convenient and lasting method of putting a rod together. The pieces are the better of being tied together, as, if they are not,

JOINING OF THE ROD.

they may slip. For this purpose, small wire catches should be put at the bottom and top of each piece.

A well-made rod, when put up, should yield slightly from a little above the hand to the top, and if intended to be used with one hand should balance about a foot above the hand; if intended to be used with both hands, about a foot farther up. The facility of casting with a well-balanced rod is very great, as the part of the rod below the hand acts as a lever.

The reel is usually attached to the rod by rings, which is undoubtedly the most convenient plan, as it can be taken off at pleasure. In a one-handed rod, the reel should be as close to the butt end as possible, as its leverage will be greater there; in a double-handed rod, sufficient room must be left below the reel for the hand. When the weight of the butt end and reel together are not in themselves sufficient to balance a rod, lead should be added till it balance at the proper place.

Rings are indispensable to a rod in order to convey the line from the reel to the point. A difference of opinion exists as to whether they should be fixed or movable. For our part, if they could be fixed so as not to move, we would prefer them that way, as they let off the line much more easily; but they generally have just sufficient stiffness to be troublesome. When they come into contact with anything, they are knocked over and remain so; and unless the angler notice it, the first fish will break his line.

When treating of the different branches of angling, we will mention the size and description of rod most suitable for each; but the size of rod we have advocated for fly-fishing is so much shorter than usual, that it may with great propriety be objected to, as being unsuitable for any other kind of fishing. To obviate this as much as possible, we have a joint made in our fly-rod about a foot from the butt end, and carry with us a spare butt of about four feet in length. This can be attached to the basket without the angler suffering the least inconvenience, or may be made with joints, which will render it more portable. When wishing to change from fly to bait, we take off the short butt and put on the long one, and have then a rod suitable for any purpose.

To keep a rod in good order, and render it impervious to wet, it should be varnished occasionally. If any part of it is made of bamboo, this should be done every three or four times it is used, as the varnish will not adhere to the skin of the cane, but cracks off in casting. For this purpose spirit varnish is generally used, which may be had of any fishing-tackle maker or druggist, and should be applied with a brush.

Reels.—The best reels are those made of brass, and with a plain wheel. Some anglers prefer the multiplier, because it rolls up the line more quickly,

REELS.

and others the rack, because it presents a greater resistance to the running off of the line : but these advantages are counterbalanced by their liability to go wrong, particularly the multiplier ; and we have known anglers who have lost a salmon by the rack catching at a critical moment. A plain wheel will sometimes allow the line to run off too freely, but this is the angler's fault, who, in playing a trout, should regulate the amount of stress to be laid on it by the hand entirely. Reels have been greatly improved in shape of late years ; they are now made much deeper, and not so broad, thus allowing the line to be run off more easily, and be wound up more quickly. The size of the reel should always bear some proportion to the size of the rod. A large reel seems quite out of place on a small rod, and *vice versâ*.

Lines are now usually made by a machine, and if care be taken in their construction, they can be made much better in this manner than by the hand. They can be bought at such a moderate price, that it is not worth any angler's trouble making them for himself. They are made of horse-hair, or a mixture of hair and silk ; those made of hair entirely are more durable than any other kind, as they are not so liable to rot as all lines are of which silk forms a component part. The latter, however, are stronger for their bulk, and are much more easily thrown—two considerable advantages. Lines made entirely of silk, prepared in some patent manner, are now in very common use, and seem likely to supersede every other kind. They are very strong, and are more easily thrown than any kind of line, but, like all lines made of silk, they will rot unless dried after being wet. As to the length of line, the angler should be guided entirely by the size of the river he intends fishing in. For small streams, twenty yards will be quite sufficient, but in first-class rivers and lochs three times that quantity will be necessary.

After the ordinary winch-line, it is usual to have a casting-line of horse-hair loosely twisted, or triple gut. Some anglers prefer the hair because they think it lighter, which, however, is a mistake, as gut is stronger for its weight than any material the angler can use, and is also heavier for its bulk, which is a great assistance to casting.

Gut.—This article is made from the entrails of the silk-worm before it casts its silk, and is principally manufactured in Spain, Portugal, Italy, and Sicily. Of all the materials used by the angler, it is the one which it is most difficult to procure good, and which it is most necessary should be so. For angling in clear water, inhabited by cunning, cautious trout, *fine thin gut is absolutely necessary for success*, and we think that anglers in Scotland are in general not sufficiently aware of the importance of fine gut. An immense quantity is imported annually, put up in hanks of about a hundred threads each. So far as we can judge, a good deal appears to be spoilt in the manufacture. As it is made at present, nine hanks out of ten are totally unfit for fine trouting purposes, and even the very finest hanks seldom contain more than twenty threads fit for dressing flies or bait-hooks upon. The first angler who travels in Spain should try to prevail upon the Spaniards to pay a little more attention to the manufacture of this article; it would amply repay them for their trouble, as they would get three times the price for it. Meantime all anglers should use none but the very finest threads, and if they continue doing so, coarse gut will become valueless, and the demand will soon influence the manufacture. We are informed by an importer that gut used to be made much better, but that the price has fallen so low, that it will not remunerate for the trouble required to make it fine; so that anglers have themselves to blame.

The qualities good gut should possess are roundness, transparency, and thinness. Unless gut is round it glitters in the sun, which renders it useless to the angler; it must also be perfectly free from that white glossy appearance which round gut frequently has, and which renders it more easily seen than clear gut of twice the thickness. Thinness, however, is the great desideratum, as the thinner it is, there is the less chance of the trout detecting it. Some anglers, particularly those in the North, seem to think that gut cannot be had too thick, whereas the reverse is the case—it cannot be had too fine.

Of late years, fishing-tackle manufacturers have been in the habit of reducing the size of gut, which is done by drawing it through a machine, and paring away a considerable portion of the gut. By this means it may be made of any thinness, but it injures the texture of the gut, and destroys its transparency, and it is certainly better if it can be had sufficiently fine without reducing. Gut prepared in this manner is also very expensive; costing from ten to sixteen shillings a hank.

All gut is more or less of a clear colour, which glitters in the sun, and in order to divest it of this it requires to be stained. The colour of the dye used is of little consequence; the object being to render it of a dull colour, and this may be best accomplished by dyeing it of a bluish-green. This dye may be made by boiling a handful of logwood in a pint of water, and adding copperas till it is of the required colour. A piece of copperas about half the size of a pea will be sufficient; if too much is put in, it will make it quite blue. The gut should be put into the liquid when cold, and allowed to remain till it is of the required colour.

Gut plays a very important part in the formation of all trouting tackle: hooks of every description should be dressed upon it; and all casting-lines, and, indeed, every part of the line that is intended to touch the water, should be made of this material.

After the ordinary winch line, there should be a casting-line composed of seven or eight lengths of triple-gut twisted together. This can only be done properly by a machine for the purpose, which may

THE CASTING-LINE.

be had in any fishing-tackle shop. Only the longest threads should be selected for this purpose, and they should be as nearly as possible of one thickness. Before attaching them to the machine they should be soaked in cold water for half-an-hour, or they will be certain to break. After the lengths are twisted, they may be joined together according to the angler's taste, taking care that they taper from one end to the other. The most secure method of joining them is with the single slip-knot, lapping the ends over with well-waxed silk thread; a little spirit varnish makes all secure. Another way of joining them is by whipping the ends together with silk; this is the neater plan of the two, but it is continually giving way, and requires to be done over again; so that, unless the angler makes up his own tackle, he will find it exceedingly troublesome; anglers practising this method should always keep the joinings well varnished. After the triple-gut line, there should be four or five lengths of picked gut, tapered in thickness to where the fly or bait tackle is attached; these should be joined together by a common knot. Instead of fastening the fly or bait cast to this by a loop, as is usually done, it is better to fasten it by a knot, as it is neater, and makes less show in the water.

There is nothing so apt to slip as gut, and therefore the knot by which to tie the threads together is of some importance. The water knot is made by laying the two ends together, rolling them round the forefinger of the left hand, and passing one thread and the adjoining end through the loop thus formed; this is called the single water-knot, and is very neat, but apt to slip. The double water-knot is done in the same way; but the ends are passed twice through instead of once, making a very firm knot, but rather clumsy. The single slip-knot is made by laying the ends together, and simply knotting the one round the other; in the right direction it will hold together, but may be separated by pulling the short ends. The double slip-knot is so far the same; but in knotting the threads round each other, the ends are passed twice through instead of once: this, if properly done, makes a neat and firm joining, and is the one we always use. Before knotting, gut should be well soaked in cold water.

Hooks.—The two great points to be attended to in the selection of hooks are the bend, and the temper and durability of the wire. Great diversity of opinion exists as to what sort of bend is best adapted for hooking, and in order to please every one, a variety of bends are made: these are the round, Limerick, Kirby, and sneck bends. The two last may be dismissed at once, as they are not a whit better adapted for hooking than the ordinary round bend, and are much more difficult to bait. The main point, as we have already stated, being to hook a fish, the round bend appears to be the best adapted for that purpose. It is an error to suppose

HOOKS. 49

that because the point of the Limerick is more turned out, it is therefore more likely to take a hold when the angler strikes; on the contrary, the more the point of the hook is turned out, the less is the chance of hooking; there is certainly a greater probability of the point of the hook coming into contact with the mouth of the fish, but it merely grazes it and then starts off. The reason of this is, that when the angler pulls, the pressure upon the point does not pull it straight in, but sideways. The accompanying illustration will assist to explain this.

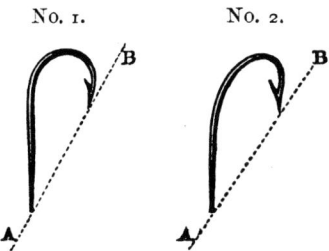

No. 1 is a round bent hook of the shape we use; No. 2 is a Limerick of the ordinary bend. When the point of a hook comes in contact with anything, the line being attached to the end of the shank, the pressure takes place in the direction of the straight line B A, so that in No. 1 the pressure will be almost in the same direction as the point; whereas in No. 2 it will be very nearly at right angles to the point, requiring three times the force to fix it, and rendering it exceedingly liable to start off and merely graze the mouth of the fish. As a proof of this, if the angler is using hooks which are not sufficiently tempered, he will frequently, after having fished for some time, find them bent out in the point, showing that the pull was so much off the straight line, that the force which was sufficient to bend the wire, was not enough to fix the hook. Whenever this is observed, the angler should restore the hook to its original shape by biting it between his teeth, as it will never catch a fish in that state. The point of the hook must not lie in exactly the same line as B A, because if it does, when it comes in contact with the mouth of a fish it will hardly take any hold at all; it must be so much off the line B A, that when it comes against anything it will press into it. In order to understand what we mean, the reader should take two dressed hooks of the same shapes as Nos. 1 and 2, and pull them against some soft substance, when he will at once see the force of these remarks.

We believe that with a fly dressed upon a hook of No. 1 bend, we could catch at least three trout for two we could catch with a fly dressed on a hook bent as No. 2, out of an equal number of rises. There are numbers of anglers who are of the same opinion, and would not use a Limerick hook on any account; and we have met with professional anglers, ready enough in general to accept of any kind of tackle, who absolutely refused to take Limerick hooks, as being of no use. Some anglers shorten the shanks of their hooks considerably, but this is highly objectionable, as it has exactly the same effect as having the point turned out, and if carried to any extent, renders the chances of hooking a trout exceedingly small.

The round bent hooks manufactured by Bartlett and Son, and Addlington and Hutchinson, can generally be depended upon for temper and durability of wire. The hooks of neither of these makers are exactly of the proper shape, being rather too much turned out in the points. Addlington's small sizes are, without exception, the best that are made, as they neither bend nor break, but are somewhat difficult to get, as few fishing-tackle makers keep them. Bartlett's small sizes are liable to bend (a very bad fault), but the same objection does not apply to his large sizes, which we prefer to Addlington's, the latter maker's hooks, from No. 9 upwards, being too thick in the wire. It is a great improvement to get them japanned in the same way as the Limerick hooks, for if left with the blue steel exposed they are exceedingly liable to rust.

Bartlett numbers his hooks from $1\frac{1}{2}$, the largest size, to 17, the smallest. Addlington's numbers are from the largest trouting size to oo, the smallest. Being better acquainted with Bartlett's hooks than any others, when we speak of hooks in the subsequent parts of this volume the reader will understand that it is his sizes to which we allude. The following numbers of Bartlett and Addlington are about the same size :—

Bartlett's Nos. . 1 2 3 4 5 6 7 8 9 10 11 12 13 14
Addlington's Nos. 12 11 10 9 8 7 6 5 4 3 2 1 0 ∞

Basket-pannier or Creel.—The most elegantly shaped baskets are those made of split willows, usually called "French made." For the size of basket every angler should be guided by the quantity of fish he expects to capture; nothing looks worse than a few trout half-hidden with grass in the bottom of a large basket. It will be found an improvement to attach a strap to the back of the basket, by which the angler may strap on his waterproof coat; this has the double advantage of being the most convenient mode of carrying it, and of acting as a kind of cushion between the basket and the back.

Landing or Minnow Net.—The meshes of the landing-net should be made sufficiently small to admit of its being employed for capturing minnows. Nets are not much used in Scotland for landing trout, as our rivers in general have plenty of smooth sloping banks, and using a net in such would rather diminish the pleasure of landing a fish. But in lochs a landing-net is indispensable, and even in rivers, if the banks are steep, or the sides weedy, it will be found a very great convenience. Under any circumstances, if the angler has an attendant to carry his basket—which we strongly advise all who angle for pleasure to have—he should have a landing-net with him, as even though he should not require it for trout, he may meet with a shoal of minnows, and feel disposed to try minnow-fishing. Nets are now made with jointed hoops, which fold up and can be put in the basket or pocket; the handles also are made with numerous joints, or in telescope fashion—the one slipping into the other—so that they take up very little room.

Fishing Pocket-book.—In order to afford ample room for the accommodation of every kind of tackle, this article should be large—at least six or seven inches long by five or six wide. It should have numerous pockets, and also divisions of parchment to keep the tackle separate. Keeping flies in a book squeezes and destroys them, and the preferable plan is to keep them in an oblong tin box, which should be from five to six inches long by four or five wide, and which may be made with a division in the middle and to open at both sides; it should also be furnished with slips of paper to keep the fly-casts separate.

Lastly, in regard to tackle, we advise anglers,

before putting past flies or lines, to dry them previously, and to have everything connected with their angling equipment of the very best material; it will be found a great assistance to successful fishing, and also the most economical plan in the end.

CHAPTER IV.

ARTIFICIAL FLY-FISHING.

FLY-FISHING has always been, and we believe always will be, the favourite method of angling; and deservedly so. Few who have once owned its sway are capable of resisting its attractions. What golden memories of the past it recalls! What bright visions of the future it portrays! And when May comes, that month pre-eminently the fly-fisher's, with its bright sunny mornings and soft southern breezes, once more, unencumbered with anything save a light rod and small box of flies, the angler wends his way to some favourite stream. Once more with elastic tread he climbs the mountain's brow, and having gained the summit, what a prospect meets his gaze! There, far as the eye can reach, rises into the blue sky summit after summit of the heath-clad hills, while underneath lie the grassy slope and luxuriant meadow, the green cornfield and waving wood, and winding and circling among all like a silver thread lies the far-stretching stream in all its beauty. There is nothing to break the solitude save the plaintive bleating of the sheep or the crow of the moorcock. As the angler descends, the music of the song-bird meets his ear from every bush, and the groves resound with the cooing of the wood-pigeon or the soft notes of the cuckoo. And now he approaches the scene of his anticipated triumph. There are the deep rocky pool and racing shallow, the whirling eddy and rippling stream. Now it pauses as if to enjoy the glory of the prospect, then rushes impetuously forward, as if eager to drink in the grandeur of some new scene. Now it foams over rocks, and then meanders slowly between green banks. Everything seems endowed with life to welcome the return of summer. The very river is alive with leaping trout. Everything tends to cheer the angler's heart and encourage his hopes. No wonder that with Sir Henry Wotton he finds "fly-fishing" a "cheerer of the spirits, a tranquilliser of the mind, a calmer of unquiet thoughts, a diverter of sadness."

And then the art itself is lively and graceful. Look at the angler as he approaches some favourite spot. See him as he observes the monarch of the pool regaling himself on the incautious insect that sports in fancied security upon the surface. Inwardly he vows that it shall be avenged. Cautiously he approaches, concealing himself by kneeling or keeping behind some bush, lest by any chance his

PRE-EMINENCE OF FLY-FISHING.

expected prey should discover him and so be warned. Gracefully wheeling his long line behind, he lays his flies down softly as a snow-flake just above the desired spot. A moment of expectancy succeeds, the flies approach the very place where the trout was last seen. Look at the angler how, with keen eye, he watches to strike with alert hand the moment he either feels or sees the least movement. There is a stoppage of the line and an instantaneous movement of the angler's wrist, and the trout is fast. At first he shakes his head as if surprised and bewildered at the unwonted interference with his liberty, but gradually awakening to a sense of the danger of his position, he collects his scattered energies and makes a gallant fight for liberty; frequently he will leap in the air several times as if to ascertain the character of his opponent, and then make a frantic rush; but the figure on the bank follows him like a shadow, and at last, strength and hope both exhausted, he turns on his side and becomes an easy prey, leaving the angler to contemplate the speckled sides of his captive with satisfaction, and to congratulate himself on having achieved such a feat with a tiny hook and tackle like a gossamer.

The victory, however, is not always with the angler—more frequently the other way; often at the last moment, just as he is putting out his hand to secure his prize, the trout makes a bolt and is gone, leaving the disappointed artist the picture of blank dismay, and in a very unenviable frame of mind; indeed, of all the trials of the temper which occur in the ordinary course of life, there is none to compare with that of losing a good trout at the last moment, and anglers have various ways of giving vent to their pent-up feelings, depending upon their peculiar idiosyncrasy. But of all the different means of relief there is perhaps none at once so satisfactory and so reprehensible as that referred to by a late great humorist, who, if not an angler, was the friend and associate of anglers:—

> "The flask frae my pocket
> I poured into the socket,
> For I was provokit unto the last degree;
> And to my way o' thinkin',
> There's naething for 't but drinkin',
> When a trout he lies winkin' and lauchin' at me."

Everything combines to render fly-fishing the most attractive of all the branches of the angler's art. The attempt to capture trout which are seen to rise at natural flies is in itself an excitement which no other method possesses. Then the smallness of the hook and the fineness of the tackle necessary for success increase the danger of escape, and consequently the excitement and pleasure of the capture; and for our own part we would rather hook, play, and capture a trout of a pound weight with fly than one of a pound and a half with minnow or worm, where the hooks being larger there is less chance of their losing their hold, and the gut being stronger there is less risk of its breaking. Fly-fishing is also the cleanest and most elegant and gentlemanly of all the methods of capturing trout. The angler who practises it is saved the trouble of working with worms, of catching, keeping alive, and salting minnows, or searching the river's banks for the natural insect. Armed with a light single-handed rod and a few flies, he may wander from county to county, and kill trout wherever they are to be found.

One advantage fly-fishing possesses above any other mode is, that it is equally applicable to all waters, be they silent lakes, slow-running rivers, or roaring streams, rendering it the most valuable of all lures to the angler. In the first chapter of this volume, it was mentioned that at least twelve pounds weight of trout might be captured almost any day during the angling season, and for three months it is by fly alone that this must be accomplished. There are few anglers aware of the service the artificial fly is capable of rendering if properly used. James Baillie, whom we have already introduced to the reader, but whose hazel rod and string tied to the top of it were familiar to all those in the habit of frequenting Leader or Gala, maintained himself and family from March to November by fly-fishing exclusively. We believe this notable person killed on an average from twelve to fourteen pounds at each excursion, and, being in delicate health, he only fished for four or five hours a day.

If our amateur friends had to make their living by fly-fishing, there are few of them we would care for dining with often.

Besides being the most attractive and valuable, artificial fly-fishing is the most difficult branch of the angler's art, and this is another reason of the preference accorded to it, since there is more merit, and therefore more pleasure, in excelling in what is difficult. An opinion, however, has of late years been gaining ground, that worm-fishing in a clear water is more difficult than fly-fishing. This opinion has been supported by Mr. Stoddart, who says—"It may perhaps startle some, and those no novices in the art, when I declare, and offer moreover to prove, that worm-fishing for trout requires essentially more address and experience, as well as a better knowledge of the habits and instincts of the trout, than fly-fishing. I do not, be it observed, refer to the practice of this branch of the art as it is followed in hill-burns and petty rivulets, neither do I allude to it as pursued after heavy rains in flooded and discoloured waters; my affirmation bears solely upon its practice as carried on during the summer months in the southern districts of Scotland, when the rivers are clear and low, and the skies bright and warm." *

This is an opinion from which we entirely dissent, and though Mr. Stoddart offers to prove his assertion, he does not attempt doing so. That

* Stoddart's *Angler's Companion*, chapter vi. page 106.

DIFFICULTY OF FLY-FISHING.

there are fewer worm-fishers who meet with success when the waters are clear, than there are fly-fishers who meet with success when the waters are coloured, we admit. But between fly-fishing when the waters are swollen after rain, or as it is practised among unwary fish in Highland streams, and fly-fishing in our much-fished southern streams, when the waters are clear, we draw the same distinction as Mr. Stoddart does between worm-fishing in a coloured water and a clear one; and the number of fly-fishers who meet with success under the circumstances just mentioned is exceedingly limited.

In trouting with the minnow, worm, or natural fly, the angler has the real fish, worm, or insect, with which to entice the trout, but in fly-fishing he has, by means of a few feathers, to deceive the wary keen-sighted fish, and make it believe that his imitation is a natural fly either alive or dead. Any one will at once see that this is the more difficult, and that to prevail upon a trout to seize a reality does not afford room for the exercise of so much skill as to prevail upon the same trout to seize an imitation. Hence fly-fishing, in the same condition of water, requires more address than angling with the worm, or any other known method; and consequently, fly-fishing in a clear low water is, beyond comparison, the most difficult of all the branches of the angler's art, and should therefore rank highest as sport.

This, however, is not an art that can be learned in a day, or so easily as some seem to imagine. A beginner becomes enamoured of fly-fishing. For six weeks he grinds at Walton and all the other authorities upon the subject, and having equipped himself with all the paraphernalia for waging a war of extermination upon the finny tribe, he rolls his hat round with cast after cast of flies, which bear a far greater resemblance to humble-bees than river insects; and thus accoutred, sets out to put his acquired information in practice. Arrived at the river-side he finds his mistake: if the water be swollen, and of the dark porter colour so celebrated among anglers, he may be rewarded with the capture of a few trout; but if it be clear, he plies his lure to the terror and alarm of almost every trout in the water, and returns, if not with an empty basket, at least with a very light one, to confirm the prevailing opinion that it is of no use fishing when the water is clear. If this opinion were correct, it would limit the time when angling could be successfully practised to a few weeks in the season, and sometimes to a few days; but fortunately for the angler it is not correct, being merely the natural result of a mode of angling which ignores the habits and instincts of the trout. Trout are just as much inclined to feed when the waters are clear as when they are coloured. In a clear water they may be seen rising in immense numbers at the natural insect, showing that they are not inclined to starve in these circumstances.

When the water is of a dark colour, it conceals the angler from view, and disguises his tackle, and so he meets with fair sport. If the body of water, though clear, is sufficiently large to conceal him from the sight of the trout, as in Tweed, Tay, and other first-class streams, he may still meet with tolerable success. But in all our small rivers and waters, when they are low and clear, not one angler out of twenty meets with much sport, and the reason of it is, because the clearness of the water either allows the trout to see him, or enables them to detect the artificial nature of his lure; and to meet these difficulties as far as possible is the great object to be aimed at in fly-fishing.

The great error of fly-fishing, as usually practised, and as recommended to be practised by books, is that the angler fishes down stream, whereas he should fish up.

We believe we are not beyond the mark in stating that ninety-nine anglers out of a hundred fish down with the artificial fly; they never think of fishing in any other way, and never dream of attributing their want of success to it. Yet we are prepared to prove, both in theory and practice, that this is the greatest reason of their want of success in clear waters. In all our angling excursions we have only met one or two amateurs and a few professionals, who fished up stream with the fly, and used it in a really artistic manner. If the wind is blowing up, anglers will occasionally fish up the pools—(as for fishing up a strong stream they never think of it)—but even then they do not do it properly, and meet with little better success than if they had followed their usual method. They will also, if going to some place up a river, walk up, not fish up to it—their plan being to go to the top of a pool, and then fish it down, never casting their line above them at all.

We shall now mention in detail the advantages of fishing up, in order to show its superiority over the old method.

The first and greatest advantage is, that the angler is unseen by the trout. Trout, as is well known, keep their heads up stream; they cannot remain stationary in any other position. This being the case, they see objects above and on both sides of them, but cannot discern anything behind them, so that the angler fishing down will be seen by them twenty yards off, whereas the angler fishing up will be unseen, although he be but a few yards in their rear. The advantages of this it is impossible to over estimate. No creatures are more easily scared than trout; if they see any object moving on the river's bank, they run into deep water, or beneath banks and stones, from which they will not stir for some time. A bird flying across the water, or the shadow of a rod, will sometimes alarm them; and nothing con-

ADVANTAGES OF FISHING UP STREAM.

nected with angling is more certain than this, that if the trout see the angler, they will not take his lure. He may ply his minnow in the most captivating manner, may throw his worm with consummate skill, or make his flies light softly as a gossamer—all will be unavailing if he is seen by his intended victim.

The next advantage of fishing up we shall notice, is the much greater probability of hooking a trout when it rises. In angling down stream, if a trout rises and the angler strikes, he runs a great risk of pulling the flies straight out of its mouth; whereas, in fishing up, its back is to him, and he has every chance of bringing the hook into contact with its jaws. This, although it may not seem of great importance to the uninitiated, tells considerably when the contents of the basket come to be examined at the close of the day's sport; indeed, no angler would believe the difference unless he himself proved it.

Another advantage of fishing up is, that it does not disturb the water so much. Let us suppose the angler is fishing down a fine pool. He, of course, commences at the top, the place where the best trout, and those most inclined to feed, invariably lie. After a few casts he hooks one, which immediately runs down, and by its vagaries, leaping in the air, and plunging in all directions alarms all its neighbours, and it is ten to one if he gets another rise in that pool. Fishing up saves all this. The angler commences at the foot, and when he hooks a trout, pulls it down, and the remaining portions of the pool are undisturbed. This is a matter of great importance, and we have frequently, in small streams, taken a dozen trout out of a pool, from which, had we been fishing down, we could not possibly have got more than two or three.

The last advantage of fishing up is, that by it the angler can much better adapt the motions of his flies to those of the natural insect. And here it may be mentioned as a rule, that the nearer the motions of the artificial flies resemble those of the natural ones under similar circumstances, the greater will be the prospects of success. Whatever trout take the artificial fly for, it is obvious they are much more likely to be deceived by a natural than by an unnatural motion.

No method of angling can imitate the hovering flight of an insect along the surface of the water, now just touching it, then flying a short distance, and so on; and for the angler to attempt by any motion of his hand to give his flies a living appearance is mere absurdity. The only moment when trout may mistake the angler's fly for a real one in its flight, is the moment it first touches the water; and in this respect fishing down possesses equal advantages with fishing up. But this is the only respect, and in order to illustrate this, we shall give a brief description of fly-fishing as usually practised down stream.

The angler, then, we shall suppose, commences operations at the head of a pool or stream, and throwing his flies as far as he can across from where he is standing, raises his rod and brings them gradually to his own side of the water. He then steps down a yard or two, repeats the process, and so on. Having dismissed the idea that the angler can imitate the flight of a living fly along the surface of the water, we must suppose that trout take the artificial fly for a dead one, or one which has fairly got into the stream and lost all power of resisting. A feeble motion of the wings or legs would be the only attempt at escape which a live fly in such a case could make. What then must be the astonishment of the trout, when they see the tiny insect which they are accustomed to seize as it is carried by the current towards them, crossing the stream with the strength and agility of an otter? Is it not much more natural to throw the flies up, and let them come gently down as any real insect would do?

In addition to drawing their flies across the stream, some anglers practise what is called playing their flies, which is done by a jerking motion of the wrist, which imparts a similar motion to the fly. Their object in doing this is to create an appearance of life, and thus render their flies more attractive. An appearance of life is certainly a great

ARTIFICIAL FLY-FISHING.

temptation to a trout, but it may be much better accomplished by dressing the flies of soft materials, which the water can agitate, and thus create a natural motion of the legs or wings of the fly, than by dragging them by jumps of a foot at a time across and up a roaring stream. Trout are not accustomed to see small insects making such gigantic efforts at escape, and therefore it is calculated to awaken their suspicions.

We believe that all fly-fishers fishing down must have noticed, that apart from the moment of alighting, they get more rises for the first few yards of their flies' course than in the whole of the remainder; and that when their flies fairly breast the stream they seldom get a rise at all. The reason of this is clear :—for the first few feet after the angler throws his flies across the stream they swim with the current; the moment, however, he begins to describe his semicircle across the water, they present an unnatural appearance, which the trout view with distrust. Experienced fly-fishers following the old method, who have observed this, and are aware of the great importance of the moment their flies alight, cast very frequently, only allowing their flies to float down a few feet, when they throw again. We have seen some Tweedside adepts fill capital baskets in this way; but, as we have before stated, it will only succeed when the water is coloured, or when there is a body of clear water sufficiently large to conceal the angler from view; and even then he may have much better sport by fishing up. The angler drawing his flies across and up stream will catch trout, and this is the strongest evidence that trout are not such profound philosophers as the notions of some would lead us to suppose. But though he does catch trout, they are in general the very smallest. Indeed, the advantages of fishing up are in nothing more apparent than in the superior size of the trout captured. We believe they will average nearly double the size of those caught with the same flies fishing down, and though generally not so large as those taken with the worm, they are not much behind them, and we almost invariably kill a few larger trout in a river with the fly than with the worm.

Though our remarks in this chapter have principally reference to angling in small rivers, where fishing up is *essential* to success, the same arguments hold good in every size or colour of water in a less degree, as, even though the trout cannot see the angler, the other advantages which we have mentioned are still in his favour.

If we were fishing a large river when it was dark-coloured, and required to wade deep, we should fish down, because the fatigue of wading up would, under such circumstances, become a serious drawback. In such a case we fish in the following manner :—Throwing our flies, partly up and partly across from where we are standing, we allow them to swim down a yard or two, when we cast again, never allowing them to go below that part of the stream opposite us. But though the angler gets over the ground as quickly this way, and casts as often, as if he were fishing up, yet he has not the same chance, because if a trout catches sight of his flies just as he is lifting them, their sudden abstraction may deter it from taking them on their again alighting; whereas in fishing up the angler casts a yard or two farther up every time, so that every trout may see his flies at the moment they alight.

The reader must not suppose that fishing up is all that is necessary for success; on the contrary, the angler may throw his flies up stream, and know less of the art of fly-fishing, and catch fewer trout, than his neighbour who is fishing down. The mere fact of an angler throwing his flies up stream is no proof that he is a fly-fisher. Of those who fish down stream some catch more and some less, and in like manner with those fishing up, one may catch three times as many as another, depending upon the particular method they adopt; and unless the reader pays *strict* attention to the details which will be mentioned subsequently, we are afraid he will not derive much benefit. Fishing up is *much more* difficult than fishing down, requiring more practice, and a better acquaintance with the habits of the trout; and we believe that a mere novice would, in a large water, catch more trout by fishing down than up, because the latter *requires more nicety* in casting. But to attain anything like eminence in fly-fishing, the angler *must* fish up, and all beginners should *persevere* in it, even though they meet with little success at first, and they will be amply rewarded for their trouble.

The only circumstance in which fishing down has the advantage of fishing up, is when the water is so dark or deep that the fish would not see, or if they did see, would not have time to seize the flies unless they moved at a slower rate than the stream. We think that this rarely applies to angling for river trout, as when inclined to feed upon flies they are generally on the outlook for them, but it does apply to salmon and sea-trout fishing. Both these fish lie in strong deep water, and as they are not accustomed to feed upon flies, they are not on the outlook for them; so that if the salmon-fisher were to throw his flies up stream, they would come down at such a rate that the salmon would never see them. Besides which, it is obvious that whatever salmon take the angler's fly for, they cannot take it for anything they have seen before, and therefore there is no reason for supposing they can detect anything unnatural in its motion.

We have devoted this chapter principally to the errors of fly-fishing as generally practised, and we hope we have succeeded in convincing the reader of the truth of our observations; but as we have frequently endeavoured in vain by *vivâ voce* demonstration to persuade anglers to fish up, we have no doubt numbers will adhere to their own way. As no amount of mere argument will convince such, we offer to find two anglers, who in a water suitable for showing the superiority of fishing up, will be more successful than any three anglers fishing down after the ordinary method.

We have just given the same reasons for fishing up stream as in our first edition, because upon this point there can be nothing new; and are as ready as ever to find anglers who are prepared to do battle on their behalf, on the terms just stated; but while one or two have come forward to dispute the theory, none have accepted our challenge and come forward to dispute the practice. One reviewer —the only objector we recollect of who gives a reason—says, "that so long as streams run down, carrying the food of the fish with them, so long should anglers fish down." This seems said purely for the sake of appearing to give a reason; and while his premises are undeniably correct, we entirely dissent from his conclusions. Streams certainly run down and carry the food of the trout with them, but along with that food they do not carry an apparition in the shape of an angler with rod and line upon the bank; and as nothing will familiarise them to such an apparition, we draw the conclusion that that apparition had better keep out of sight and fish up stream. Moreover, the fact that the natural food floats down is anything but a reason that the artificial lure in imitation of that food should be pulled up.

We must confess, however, that fishing up stream with fly has not been adopted by a large portion of the angling community, and that for various reasons. In spite of the strong manner in which we cautioned our readers about the difficulties of fishing up stream, numbers who read the arguments for it, and were struck with the soundness of the theory, thought they saw at a glance the cause of their previous want of success, and that in future the result would be different. Having equipped themselves *à la Practical Angler*, and even taken a copy of that excellent work in their pockets, they started with high hopes on their new career, but the result was not different, and after one or two trials with no better success, not a few have condemned fishing up stream as erroneous and ourselves as impostors; though we imagine the fault lies with themselves. We have met anglers fishing down stream—and this is no suppositious case, but one which we have seen over and over again—with a copy of this volume in their pockets, who complained that they had got everything herein recommended and were getting no sport. On pointing out to them that there was one important mistake they were committing, in fishing down stream instead of up, they stated that when they came to a pool they fished it up—that is to say, they first walked down the pool and showed themselves to the trout, and then commenced to fish for them.

> "The trout within yon wimplin' burn
> Glides swift, a silver dart;
> And safe beneath the shady thorn
> Defies the angler's art."

John Younger objects to this as incorrect, but we rather think that Burns is right, and the angler wrong; as it is evident the poet alludes to a trout that has caught sight of the angler, and safe he is at least *pro tem.*, as our pupils, who first frighten the fish by walking down a pool-side and then fish up it, will find to their cost.

Others object to fishing up stream, as requiring too frequent casting, being too fatiguing, and because they have been accustomed to fish down, and would prefer fishing in that way, even though they do not catch so many trout. If any angler prefers catching five pounds weight of trout fishing down stream, to ten pounds weight fishing up, we may wonder at his taste, but it is no concern of ours. Our duty is to point out how most trout can be captured in a given time; and that is by fishing up stream, and such is now the method adopted by all the best fly-fishers of the day.

Those anglers who have adopted fishing up stream are principally those who were adepts in the old system, and who were possessed of all the nicety in casting and other knowledge so essential to successful up-stream fishing.

SUMMARY OF THE ART.

The art of fly-fishing—or fishing of any kind—may be summed up in knowing what to fish with, and how, when, and where to fish. We have rather transposed the arrangement, and taken part of the second division first, because it is necessary to establish whether the angler should fish up or down, before considering what he is to fish with, different tackle being necessary for the former method. In the subsequent chapters we shall return to the proper arrangement, and shall complete in its proper place the division already half finished.

CHAPTER V.

FLIES, FLY-DRESSING, ETC.

THE practice of using artificial flies has undoubtedly had its origin in the necessity for imitating insects which cannot be used in their natural state. From the first rude attempt at fly-making of some ingenious angler, the art has gone on progressing, the number of imitations always increasing, and the prevalent opinion always being that, in order to fish successfully, the angler must use an imitation of one or other of the natural insects on the water at the time. In spite of the exertions of Mr. Wilson and Mr. Stoddart to inculcate an opposite theory, this opinion is still held by the great majority of anglers in Scotland, while in England it is all but universal.

Anglers holding these views rejoice in the possession of as many different varieties of flies as would stock a fishing-book, all of which they consider imitations of so many real insects, and classify under the heads of the different months when these

ODD NOTIONS RESPECTING FLIES.

appear. They have a fly for the morning, another for noon, and another for the evening of every day in the year, and spend a great deal of time in taking off one fly, because it is a shade too dark, and a second because it is a shade too light, and a third to give place to the imitation of some insect which has just made its appearance on the water.

During the summer months it is supposed that the varieties of insects are reckoned by the thousand, and we have seen several dozens of different kinds on the water at one time, all of which are greedily devoured by the trout. Those anglers who think trout will take no fly unless it is an exact imitation of some one of the immense number of flies they are feeding on, must suppose that they know to a shade the colour of every fly on the water, and can detect the least deviation from it— an amount of entomological knowledge that would put to shame the angler himself, and a good many naturalists to boot. This opinion arises from the supposition that trout will not take anything readily unless they are accustomed to feed upon it, and consequently that they will not take a fly unless it has been on the water sufficiently long to allow them to become acquainted with it. Nothing can be more erroneous than this. Trout will take worms and grubs which they have never seen before. They will also take parr-tail readily, and they can never have seen it before; and in like manner with other things; and there is no reason why fly should be an exception.

We do not think it at all likely that trout can see the colour of a fly very distinctly. The worst light of all for seeing its colour is when it is placed between you and the sky, as the trout see it. And when the fly is rolled round by every current, and sometimes seen through the medium of a few feet of running water, the idea that they can detect its colour to a shade is highly improbable. Even granting they could, there is no reason for supposing they would reject it on that account. Flies of the same kind differ so much in colour that we could show the reader a May-fly almost black, and a May-fly almost yellow, and of all the intermediate shades.

It is singular inconsistency, that anglers, scrupulously exact about a shade of colour, draw their flies across and up stream in a way in which no natural insect was ever seen moving, as if a trout could not detect an alteration in the motion much more easily than a deviation in the colour of a fly.

The argument brought by anglers in support of these views is, that having fished unsuccessfully all the morning, they changed their flies and had good sport, or that when they were getting nothing they met with some celebrated local angler, who gave them the fly peculiar to the district, after which they met with success. We think that on most of these occasions the trout take better, not because the new fly is more to their liking, but because as the day advances they are more inclined to feed. We have frequently proved this by rechanging to our flies which at first proved unsuccessful, and have almost invariably found they were as killing as their predecessors. Other causes also operate. The thread of gut on which the fly is dressed is of more importance than the fly itself; and those professional anglers who haunt most southern streams, and whose "fail-me-never" is the only fly suitable for the water—because they expect to be well paid for it—take care to have their flies dressed on fine gut.

Such a difference does the gut make, that if an angler will take two threads of gut of the same thickness, but one of a glossy white colour, and the other clear and transparent, and dress two flies upon them exactly alike, the fly dressed on the clear gut will kill two trout for one which the fly dressed on the white gut will. The shape of the fly will also make a great difference, and really practical anglers, such as all those who make their living by it are, do not put a third of the feathers on their flies that some town-made ones have.

We have frequently got flies, which, we were assured, were exact imitations of some fly on the water at the time, and which the donors were certain would kill more trout than any other, but on trying them we did not find them so deadly as those we were using; and they killed quite as well, and sometimes better, two months before the natural fly came on the water, or two months after it was gone. We think it just possible that when a large fly, such as the green drake, remains a long time on the water, trout may recognise it, and when the waters are dark coloured and there is a strong breeze of wind, take an imitation of it more readily than any other. But in our own experience we have never found this to be the case; and though we have frequently tried this fly—so celebrated on English streams—we have never found it nearly so deadly as our usual flies, even when the water was coloured; and in clear water it failed entirely, as all large flies will, for the obvious reason that their size enables the trout to detect their artificial character. Furthermore, we have killed more trout with this imitation in the month of May, before the real insects had made their appearance, than in June, when the water was swarming with them, which we ascribe to the circumstance that trout will take a larger fly in May than in June.

This opinion would not have been maintained so long, but that there is at first sight a degree of plausibility about it, and that it does not to any great extent interfere with the successful practice of fly-fishing. What is meant for an imitation of a particular fly may occasionally do good service; not because the trout see any resemblance between

BEST COLOURS FOR FLIES.

it and the fly it is intended to imitate, but because, if the size and colour are suitable, it will just kill as well as any other. And we believe the angler who has a different fly for every day in the season will kill nearly as many trout as the angler who adheres to three or four varieties the whole season through; but he is proceeding upon an erroneous principle, and losing both labour and time.

That trout sometimes take more readily flies of one colour than another is certain, and the reason of their doing so affords room for a great deal of ingenious speculation, but it is exceedingly difficult to ascertain satisfactorily. We think that to some extent a certain colour is more deadly, because it is more readily seen. In clear waters we have rarely found a black fly surpassed by any other, and in such circumstances a black fly is very easily seen. In dark waters a yellow bodied fly, or one of dingy white colour, takes readily, being easily seen. And on Tweedside, in the month of July, just after sunset, a bright yellow fly is held in great repute, and such is more likely to attract attention than any other. Mere caprice, however, and love of variety, may be the main reasons why the trout prefer one colour to another.

A rule to be guided by on this point is of little use, as the angler can always regulate the colour of his flies by practice; and in practice it has been proved beyond doubt, that a black, brown, red, and dun-coloured fly, used together, and varied in size according to circumstances, will at any time kill as well, and even better, than the most elaborate collection arranged for every month in the year. If trout are at all inclined to rise, one or other of the above will be found inviting. It is quite clear that whatever the angler's opinion with regard to flies may be—whether he believes that he must have an imitation of some insect on the water at the time, that he must have a fly of the same colour as the majority of those on the water, or with ourselves holds neither of these opinions; if he has four flies such as those mentioned above, he cannot be very far off the mark, as these comprise all the leading colours of which insects generally are.

The opinion that it is necessary to imitate the particular fly on the water at the time has recently received the weight of Mr. Francis Francis' support, who in advocating what may be called the English theory gives a sort of side-wipe to Scotch anglers —the drift of his remarks being, that though a small assortment of flies may do well enough in Scotch streams where little fishing goes on and anglers count their takes by the dozen, it will not answer in the much-fished streams on the other side of the Border, where anglers count their takes by the brace. If Mr. Francis' views as to an exact imitation being necessary in English streams be correct, which we very much doubt, he will

MR. FRANCIS' OPINION ON FLIES.

require to find some other reason for its being unnecessary in Scotland than this. In comparing the severity of the fishing in Scotch and English streams, it must be borne in mind that the former are, as a rule, open to the public, and that the latter, as a rule, are preserved, and fished only by a favoured few. If Mr. Francis will point out any stream in England, in which he thinks it worth while to throw a fly for trout, that is more and better fished than Tweed and its tributaries, we shall be very much surprised. And on behalf of Scotch anglers we repudiate with scorn the bare idea that it requires less skill to catch a Scotch trout than an English one, or that the former in any way receives an inferior education as regards flies, etc., to his English brother. In fact, we believe that in the before-mentioned streams the education of the inhabitants is as superior to that of the inhabitants of English streams as the education of the people of the one country is admitted to be to that of the other; and supposing the most accomplished believer in the English theory—ay, even Mr. Francis himself—engaged on a mile of Tweed along with twenty or thirty Galashiels weavers (by no means an unusual number), we question if his basket at the finish would illustrate very strongly the superiority of his theory and practice. We have met English anglers even in Scotland counting their takes by the brace, and not in much danger of going wrong in their reckoning either. Having relieved our feelings of this protest on behalf of Scotch anglers and Scotch trout, we must now consider what it is necessary to imitate, or what do trout take, or rather mistake, the artificial fly for. As before stated, we believe that, deceived by an appearance of life, they take it for what it is intended to imitate—a fly or some other aquatic insect. In proof of this, artificial flies are not of much use unless the trout are at the time feeding on the natural insect. And an artificial fly will kill twenty trout for one which the feathers composing it, rolled round the hook without regard to shape, will. Nay, more; a neatly-made, natural-looking fly will, where trout are shy, kill three trout for one which a clumsy fly will; and a fly with the exposed part of the hook taken off will raise more trout than a fly with the same left on. In the first case, the trout see no resemblance in form to anything they are accustomed to feed upon, and, unless very hungry, decline to seize it. In the second case, the resemblance to nature not being so complete in the one fly as in the other, fewer trout are deceived by it. The third case shows that trout can detect that a hook is an unnatural appendage.

The great point, then, in fly-dressing, is to make the artificial fly resemble the natural insect in shape, and the great characteristic of all river insects is extreme lightness and neatness of form. Our great objection to the flies in common use is, that they are much too bushy; so much so, that there are few flies to be got in the tackle-shops which we could use with any degree of confidence in clear water. Every possible advantage is in favour of a lightly-dressed fly; it is more like a natural insect; it falls lighter on the water, and every angler knows the importance of making his fly fall gently, and there being less material about it, the artificial nature of that material is not so easily detected; and also, as the hook is not so much covered with feathers, there is a much better chance of hooking a trout when it rises. We wish to impress very strongly upon the reader the *necessity of avoiding bulky flies.*

The artificial flies in common use may be divided into two classes. There is first the winged fly, which alone, properly speaking, merits the appellation; and there is the palmer hackle or spider, by which last name we mean to call it, believing that if it resembles anything in the insect tribe, it is a spider. As a means of capturing trout, we rank them higher than the winged imitations. When trout are taking, winged flies will answer very well; and sometimes, but very rarely, we have found them more killing than spiders. But in the summer months, when trout are well fed and become lazy, or where they are much fished for, and become shy, we have found spiders much more deadly than the most tempting winged fly that can be made. Nor is it necessary to go very much out of the way to seek a reason for this: the hook is better concealed, and if made of sufficiently soft materials, the water agitates the feathers, and gives them a life-like appearance, which has a wonderful effect, and is of itself a sufficient reason for trout preferring them, without supposing, as some do, that spiders are greater rarities than flies, with a variety of other fine-spun theories.

By universal consent, feathers seem to have been fixed upon as the most suitable materials for imitating flies. Some years ago gutta percha wings were tried, but in every respect they are inferior. The selection of proper feathers requires some care; they should always be taken from the birds when in their full plumage, which is usually about Christmas. Among those considered most necessary are hackles, which are usually taken from the neck of the common cock. It is very difficult to procure them of the right colour, and still more so to procure them of the right shape. In a proper hackle the fibres should be longest at the root end, and taper gradually towards the point. It is not one cock out of twenty whose hackles merit the attention of the fly-dresser.

The hackle generally plays a very conspicuous part in the construction of trouting flies. The spider or hackle fly is made of it entirely, and in other flies it is used to imitate the legs of the insect. We, however, think the cock-hackle by no means deserving of so much attention as is bestowed upon it, being too stiff and wiry to represent the legs of an insect, and we prefer hen-hackles, or still better, the small feathers taken from the neck or outside of the wings of a variety of small birds. But these latter are not always to be had of the colour wanted, and cock-hackles are very convenient to fall back upon, but should be selected as soft in the fibre as possible. Amongst those most serviceable to the angler are the small feathers taken from the outside of the wings, as also from the neck and shoulders of the following birds:—The starling, landrail, dotterel, mavis, grey plover, golden plover, partridge, and grouse. Of the foregoing, we consider the feathers taken from the cock starling the most valuable of all to the angler. They have a rich glossy black, which no other feathers possess, and we always use them in place of the black cock-hackle. Next to them we rank the feathers of a reddish-brown colour taken from the outside of the wing of the landrail, the only feathers which take the place of the red cock-hackle; and as it is impossible to get any quantity of these sufficiently small, we frequently find it necessary to have recourse to red hackles.

The feathers of the dotterel are also held in high esteem, but all those just mentioned may with advantage be substituted for the hackle in the formation of all trouting flies and spiders. Their superiority consists in their much greater resemblance to the legs of an insect, and their extreme softness. So soft are they, that when a spider is made of one of them and placed in the water, the least motion will agitate and impart a singularly life-like appearance to it, whereas it would have no effect upon a cock-hackle. Spiders dressed of very soft feathers are more suitable for fishing up than for fishing down, as, if drawn against the stream, it runs the fibres alongside of the hook, and all resemblance to an insect is destroyed.

Killing spiders may be made of all the feathers we have mentioned, but the three following are all we consider necessary :—

1st. The Black Spider.—This is made of the small feather of the cock starling, dressed with brown silk, and is, upon the whole, the most killing imitation we know. We were first shown it by James Baillie, and have never been without one on our line ever since.

2nd. The Red Spider should be made of the small feather taken from the outside of the wing of the landrail, dressed with yellow silk, and is deserving of a very high rank, particularly in coloured water.

3rd. The Dun Spider.—This should be made of the small soft dun or ash-coloured feather, taken from the outside of the wing of the dotterel. This bird is unfortunately very scarce; but a small feather may be taken from the inside of the wing of the starling, which will make an excellent substitute.

The only objection to spiders is, that the feathers are so soft that the trout's teeth break them off, and after catching a dozen or two of trout, little is left of them but the bare dressing, rendering it necessary for the angler to change them; and if the trout are taking readily, this has to be repeated two or three times a day. For this reason we always use winged flies, when they take equally well, which, if well dressed, will last a whole day or even two. For making flies, in addition to the feathers before mentioned, the wings of the following birds are necessary:—Corn-bunting, lark, chaffinch, woodcock, and landrail. These are used to make the wings of the flies, but dubbing of some sort is also necessary to form the body, and for this purpose there is nothing better than the fur of a hare's ear, or, as it is usually called in Scotland, "hare-lug." A good hare lug will make body for five or six gross of flies of all colours, from dingy white to dark black, but the mixed dark fur is the best. The fur of the water-rat is also serviceable to the fly-dresser, and is peculiarly suitable for small flies. The three following are the winged flies to which we are most partial:—

1st. A woodcock wing with a single turn of a red hackle, or landrail feather, dressed with yellow silk, freely exposed on the body. For fishing in dark-coloured waters, this fly may be dressed with scarlet thread.

2nd. A hare-lug body, with a corn-bunting or chaffinch wing. A woodcock wing may also be put in the same body, but should be made of the small light-coloured feather taken from the inside of the wing.

3rd. The same wing as the last fly, with a single turn of a soft black hen-hackle, or small feather taken from the shoulder of the starling, dressed with dark-coloured silk.

An immense number of killing flies may be made by varying the wings and body, but nothing is gained by extending the number beyond those just mentioned, and we do not believe six more killing imitations can be manufactured. We have fished with flies of all kinds, and got flies from several of the best anglers, both amateur and professional, but have never found anything superior to these, and we can recommend them with great confidence.

For fly-dressing, in addition to the feathers, etc., just mentioned, a number of miscellaneous articles are necessary—namely, brass nippers for putting on small feathers or hackles ; a pair of fine scissors, curved at the points ; a needle for dividing wings and raising dubbing ; silk of all colours, the thinner the better, as it makes the firmer dressing ; shoemaker's wax, and a mixture of resin and burgundy pitch, to be used when the colour of the silk is intended to be shown on the fly ; hooks of all sizes, the bend to be particularly attended to. The size

METHOD OF DRESSING A SPIDER.

of hook should always bear some proportion to the size of fly, but the exact size of hook that will be most killing with a fly of a certain size is exceedingly difficult to determine. Some of the shop flies are dressed upon hooks so small, and rolled round with so much dubbing and hackle, that we would consider their chances of hooking one trout out of ten rises exceedingly problematical. We have frequently fished with a very small fly, say No. 15, and a larger fly, say No. 12, of the same kind, and found that though the smaller fly raised twice the number, it did not secure so many as the larger one. We have also tried dressing two flies of the same kind and size, one on a No. 14, and the other on a No. 12 hook. The No. 12 was of course very much exposed, notwithstanding which it did most execution. This should be done very cautiously; but by having hooks made a size thinner in the wire, they may be used one size larger with perfect safety. We have endeavoured to indicate the proper size of hook in a subsequent illustration.

Great care should be taken to select the finest and longest threads of gut for dressing flies on. When the waters are clear, fine gut is quite as necessary as good flies; the finest gut, however lightly thrown, will sometimes alarm the trout.

Dressing a spider is a much simpler operation than dressing a fly, and therefore it is better to begin with it. Having selected a thread of gut and a hook, the next thing is to choose a feather, which, to make a neat spider, must be so proportioned to the size of the hook, that the legs of the spider, when dressed, will be about the length of the hook. Before commencing, bite the end of the gut between your teeth; this flattens and makes it broader in the point, which prevents it slipping; a thing very liable to occur with small flies. Next, take the hook firmly between the forefinger and thumb of your left hand, lay the gut along its shank, and with a well-waxed silk thread, commencing about the centre of the hook, whip it and the gut firmly together, till you come to the end of the shank, where form the head by a few turns of the thread. This done, take the feather, and laying it on with the root end towards the bend of the hook, wrap the silk three or four times round it, and then cut off the root end.

What remains to be done is the most critical part of the whole operation: still holding the hook between the forefinger and thumb of your left hand, take the thread, lay it along the centre of the inside of the feather, and with the forefinger and thumb of your right hand twirl them round together till the feather is rolled round the thread; and in this state wrap it round the hook, taking care that a sufficient number of the fibres stick out to represent the legs; to effect this it will sometimes be necessary to raise the fibres with a

METHOD OF DRESSING A FLY.

needle during the operation. Having carried the feather and thread down to where you commenced, wrap the silk three or four times round the end of the feather, and if there is any left cut it off, and finish with a succession of hitch-knots, or the common whip-fastening. If the legs of the spider when dressed are too long, there is no remedy for it; cutting injures rather than improves them. This is a very rough and simple mode of dressing a spider, and does not make it so neat as if the feather were put on by a pair of nippers, but it is more natural-looking, and much more durable, as the feather is fastened on by the thread the whole way down.

A fly is more difficult to dress neatly than a spider. Having selected the gut and hook, take the feather of which you intend to make the wings, and stripping off as much as you require, fold it up, taking care that the lightest coloured side of the feather is outside, and lay it beside the other materials. It is quite common in fishing-tackle shops to see the wings put on singly—that is to say, consisting of merely one fold of the feather. This makes a beautiful fly out of the water, but when once wet, is of little further use, as the fibres run together, and form a mere thread. The wings should consist of several folds of the feather, as then they keep their original shape, wetting improving rather than injuring their appearance.

In dressing a fly, commence in the same manner

as in dressing a spider, carrying the thread up to within three or four turns of the end of the shank; then take the feathers, of which you are to form the wings, firmly between the forefinger and thumb of your right hand, lay it to the bare end of the shank, whip the thread firmly round it two or three times, and then cut off the root end of the feather as close as possible. To put on the wings neatly, and make them lie properly, is the most difficult part of fly-making, and care must be taken to lay them on so that, when fastened, they will be the proper length, as it does not do to cut them. The wings being now fastened on, but in the whole, divide them, and passing the silk between them, bring it up crossways.

So far, the dressing of all flies is alike, but the remainder of the operation depends upon whether the fly is to be dressed with a hackle or dubbing.

If it is to be made with dubbing, all that remains to be done is to take a little of it, and applying it to the silk with the forefinger and thumb of the right hand, twist them both together till the dubbing is thoroughly rolled round the silk; and in that state wrap it round the hook till the body of the fly is made, when finish as usual; then with a needle raise a few of the hairs of the dubbing, close to the head of the fly, to give it a feathery appearance.

If the fly is to be dressed with a feather or hackle, after having put on the wings lay the

METHOD OF DRESSING A FLY.

hackle on as in dressing a spider, with the root end towards the bend of the hook; fasten it on and cut off the root end. Next take hold of the end of the hackle with your brass nippers, and turn it once or twice round the hook as close under the wings as possible; then wrap the silk three or four times round it to make it secure, cut off the remainder, and carry the thread by itself down to where you intend finishing. In a large fly it will be an improvement to put on a little dubbing of the same colour as the body of the fly, after having put on the hackle. The most expeditious way of dressing flies is to dress say a dozen of one kind at a time, selecting and arranging all the materials necessary before commencing.

The following illustration shows what appearance the flies should present when finished.

The first of the accompanying flies is a spider, the second a fly dressed with dubbing, and the third a fly dressed with a hackle. The reader will observe that these flies are very light in the make; that there is not more dubbing than covers the thread; that the hackle is put on very sparingly; and that the dressing is not carried far down the hook. Anglers accustomed to shop-made flies may think this is carried to an extreme, but we have met anglers using flies with sufficient dubbing on them to have made body for half-a-dozen flies, each fly more killing than the original; and as a last advice upon flies, we advise all anglers to use them very light. The spider is made rather more bushy than is advisable at first, as the trout's teeth would otherwise tear it away too fast. After capturing a dozen trout it will be spare enough.

It is exceedingly difficult by means of written instructions to make fly-dressing intelligible to the reader; a few lessons would do more than a whole volume of instructions.

It is very difficult to dress flies neatly, and unless anglers have plenty of time to devote to it, they would act wisely in purchasing their flies from professional dressers, who will make them to any pattern; but anglers should see that they *are* dressed to pattern. Since the first edition was published, our friends have shown us flies which they bought as being the kind we recommended, and as being tied on fine gut, but which were the identical bushy flies which we have devoted so many pages to warn anglers against; and as for the gut, it was so thick and coarse as to preclude the possibility of success in anything like fine fishing. All the knowledge of the habits of the trout, all the skill, all the energy, possessed by the most accomplished angler, are merely thrown away in the use of such tackle; no angler, not even James Baillie, could fill even a small basket in clear water with such tackle. We have given illustrations for the very purpose that anglers may compare their flies with them, but it is impossible that fishing-tackle makers can take the care necessary to make proper flies, dress them on the finest gut, and sell them at the present price.

Several flies are always used together, and the method of joining them, or, as it is usually called, making up the fly-cast, is a point of some importance. The two things most necessary are neatness and firmness. We have before mentioned that the gut on which the flies are dressed should be the very finest, and it is equally necessary that the threads used to connect them be of the same description. The following illustration will assist us in explaining to the reader the proper mode of making up a fly-cast.

The thread of gut on which the tail-fly is dressed is here indicated by the letter *a;* those on which the bobs or droppers are dressed by *b* and *c.* Commence operations by joining the ends of the threads of gut *a* and *b* together; you have now a fly at both ends. Next take a thread of gut and join it to *b* a few inches above the hook, then join the end of *c* to this, and so on till you have got the required number. The gut on which the droppers are dressed thus forms a continuation of the main line, and for this reason they should be dressed on the very longest threads.

The droppers should hang down from the main line from two and a half to three inches. If the distance is increased, they are apt to become ravelled with the main line, and occasion the angler considerable loss of time. The distance between the flies should be from twenty inches to two feet. If it is greater in rough water, the angler may pass over a trout without its seeing any of them, and there is nothing in the sight of two flies at a time calculated to alarm a trout.

Some works, when giving instructions for making a fly-cast, recommend that the first dropper should depend from the main line about three inches, the second, five, and so on, always increasing the distance when a fly is added. Their object, if we understand it aright, being, that in fishing, the flies are to be drawn along the water, so that the main line does not touch it at all, but merely the flies. This discloses a very erroneous method of fly-fishing. No angler with any pretentions to skill ever allows his flies, or even his line, for yards above them, to create a disturbance in the water, nothing being more calculated to alarm a trout than seeing flies or line rippling the surface, which the flies must do if drawn along the water sufficiently fast to keep the main line out of it. A great many different methods of making up fly-casts are practised by anglers. Some append them by loops, but loops make such a show in the water that we never have one in any part of our line, and to have the droppers depended by them we consider perfectly suicidal. Others join the main line together by the single slip-knot, which is drawn asunder, and the end of the thread of gut on which the fly is dressed having had a knot put on it to prevent it from slipping, is inserted, when the knot is drawn together again. In point of neatness this is less objectionable, but is apt to slip, as all single knots are. The neatest and most secure method is the one first described, and all anglers should adopt it.

The number of flies that should be used at a time is a matter upon which great diversity of opinion exists; some anglers never use more than three, while others occasionally use a dozen. If the river is so large that the angler cannot reach the opposite bank, he may use as many as he can throw properly; but if the river can be commanded from bank to bank, the propriety, under any circumstances, of using more than three or four is exceedingly doubtful. In such cases the opposite bank is the place where most trout are to be had, and if a number of flies are used, and they are all kept in the water, justice cannot be done to the tail-fly, which alone reaches the opposite bank, and has therefore the best chance.

The fly-casts should be joined to the casting-line

by four or five lengths of picked gut, and the whole line should increase in thickness gradually from the flies to the rod; it is a great assistance to casting.

The only point connected with this subject which remains to be considered is the rod, and it is a very important one. The rod may be used either double or single-handed. If the river is large, and the angler is not wading, a double-handed rod might be advisable; if he is wading, even in a large river, a single-handed one will be sufficient; and in all rivers which can be commanded from bank to bank, either by wading or otherwise, it should always be used. For fly-fishing, where light throwing and quick striking are indispensable, a double-handed rod is an unmanageable weapon. With it the angler can neither cast with so much certainty, nor strike so instantaneously when he gets a rise, as with a light single-handed rod. It is also exceedingly difficult to regulate with it the amount of force necessary to fix the hook, the force necessary to move the rod being exceedingly apt to tear small hooks away from their hold. Besides which, it takes a much longer time to cast, and where repeated casting is necessary, this becomes a serious objection.

A light stiff single-handed rod, about ten feet long, will be amply sufficient for most waters. Those accustomed to use rods from twelve to thirteen feet may think this much too short, but a stiff rod of this length will throw a line farther than one of thirteen feet, made as supple as they usually are. And even in rods of the same stiffness, a couple of feet extra length will not enable the angler to throw much farther from him. For supposing he is using a line twice the length of his rod, he will have four feet extra length of line and two of rod, in all six feet. But then the rod in casting is never held straight out, but at an angle of about forty-five degrees; the line also makes an angle with the water, so that five feet is the utmost additional command of water gained, and this is much more than counterbalanced by the facility of casting with the small rod, and by its lightness; two feet extra length in a rod entailing at least a half more weight.

It is quite common among anglers to suppose that a twelve-foot rod will command twice as much water as one of six feet, but this is an error; and in order to explain this, it is necessary to consider in what the casting power of a rod consists. The first power in the casting of a line is the force with which it is urged forward; thus, if the angler uses a great amount of force, his line will go farther than if he uses a less amount. The forward motion is communicated to the line by the point of the rod, so that upon the rapidity with which the point of the rod moves through the air depends the motive-power applied to the line. We think the point of a six-foot rod may be sent through the air as fast as that of a twelve-foot one; and, therefore, if the angler was standing on an elevation of six feet, he could throw almost as long a line with the small rod as he could with the large one standing on a level with the water. But standing on the same level he could not do this, because with the short rod the line would come into contact with the water long before it had reached its full length; so that upon the altitude of the point of the rod, or the time the line gets to go forward without touching the water, depends the length of line that can be thrown.

Now, supposing the angler holds both rods in his hand, at a distance of five feet from the ground, the altitude of the point of the six-foot rod will be eleven feet and of the twelve-foot rod seventeen feet. But as substances fall faster every succeeding moment, instead of the times which the lines take to fall from the respective rods being in the proportion of eleven to seventeen, they will be nearly in the proportion of seven to nine; and since the length of line that can be thrown depends entirely upon the length of time it gets to go forward, seven to nine will also be nearly the proportion of the lengths of line that can be thrown. Now, if twenty-one feet is the utmost length of line that the small rod will throw, the large one will throw twenty-seven, or six feet more. Besides this, there are six feet additional length of rod. But as both rod and line are at an angle with the water, the whole gain will only be about nine feet additional command of water. Taking everything into account, the water commanded by the two rods will be very nearly in the proportion of twenty-five to thirty-five.

We are thus particular, in order to show anglers that the additional power of casting is proportionally less with every foot added, and that a ten-foot rod is really a very serviceable weapon. Even with a rod of nine feet we very rarely have occasion to exert its casting powers to their full extent. Fly-fishing, if properly and quickly done, is hard work; and the angler must on no account use a rod in the least degree heavier or longer than he can thoroughly manage with one hand.

The great essential, however, for the fly-rod is stiffness. We have already, when treating of rods, mentioned the advantages a stiff rod possesses over a supple one; and we may perhaps startle some of our readers, who are accustomed to consider a pliant rod indispensable for fly-fishing, by saying that a much stiffer rod is necessary for this branch of the art than any other. For reasons which will be afterwards shown, the flies should first fall on the water, and as little of the line with them as possible. To accomplish this, considerable force must be employed in casting, and the rod must be stopped pretty suddenly. If this is attempted with a supple rod, it would bend till it almost touched the water, and then recoil, throwing the line only a short distance. A supple rod may answer tolerably for fishing down with the wind, but for fishing up, or fishing any way either against or sideways to the wind, it is perfectly useless.

CHAPTER VI.

ON TROUTING WITH THE FLY.

HAVING in the preceding chapters expressed our opinion, that fly-fishing should be practised up stream, and having mentioned the flies and tackle most suitable for the purpose, we now request the reader's particular attention to the remainder of the subject, as being the most important part of it.

The first point which falls under consideration is the casting of the line. After having put up your rod, drawn off a sufficient quantity of line from your reel, and fastened on your flies; before commencing, soak the line and flies in the water for a few minutes, as it is no use fishing when the gut is dry, and lying in rebellious curls upon the surface; and when, should a trout take any of the flies, there is a great risk of its carrying them all away—dry gut being very brittle and apt to break at the knots. When the line is thoroughly soaked, take the rod in your right hand, raise it with sufficient force to make the line go to its full length behind, and then pausing for a moment till it has done so, with a circular motion of the wrist and arm urge the rod forward, rapidly at first, but gradually lessening the speed, so that when it stops no recoil of the point will take place. The whole motion of the rod in casting should be in the shape of a horse-shoe; and care must be taken not to urge the flies forward, till they have gone the full length behind, or you will be apt to crack them off. Many a beginner who cracks off his flies pleases himself with the idea that some trout of large dimensions has carried them away.

The line must be so thrown that the flies will fall first upon the water, and as little of the line with them as possible. If you were to fish up a strong stream, and allow the middle of your line to light first, before you could get it straight and prepared for a rise, your flies would be almost at your feet, and should a trout take one of them on their alighting—the most deadly moment in the whole cast—the chances of hooking it would be exceedingly small. It is very different if the flies light first; the line is then nearly straight from the point of the rod to the flies, and the least motion of the hand is felt almost instantaneously. Again, in fishing nooks, eddies, and comparatively still water, at the opposite sides of strong streams, if any of your line lights in the current it is dragged down, and the flies no sooner touch the water, than they are drawn rapidly away in a most unnatural manner, and without giving the trout time to seize them should they feel inclined.

In order to make the flies light first, considerable force must be employed in casting; and the rod must be kept well up; it should never be allowed to make a lower angle with the water than from forty to forty-five degrees. It is upon this point that beginners fail. Their unavailing efforts to get the line well out are entirely owing to their allowing the point of their rod to go too far down, and to their stopping it too quickly, which makes the point recoil, and stops the line in its forward motion. When the flies are just about alighting on the water, you should slightly raise the point of your rod; this checks their downward motion, and they fall much more softly.

The first advice given to beginners, in all treatises upon fly-fishing, is to acquire the art of throwing a long and light line. This practice of throwing a long line is the natural consequence of fishing down stream, and for this method of fishing it is absolutely necessary—the advantage being, that the angler is farther away from the trout, and therefore less likely to be seen. As we have already shown, this can only be accomplished in a very limited and imperfect manner by throwing a long line, whereas fishing up secures the object perfectly.

In contradistinction to the maxim of throwing a long line, we advise the angler never to use a long line when a short one will, by any possibility,

DISADVANTAGES OF A LONG LINE.

answer the purpose. The disadvantages of a long line are, that too much of it touches the water, and that it is impossible to throw it as it should be done, making the flies light first. It is also very difficult to throw it to any desired spot with certainty—to cast it neatly behind a stone or under a bank; besides which, more time is necessary to throw it, thus wasting that valuable commodity. The greatest objection to it, however, is its disadvantages in striking a trout; a long line lies curved in the water, and when the angler strikes, it is some time before the flies move; the line, in fact, requires to be straightened first. When they do move, it is slowly and without force, and there is little chance of hooking the trout. It is very different with a short line; in this case the line is almost straight from the point of the rod to the flies, and the least motion of the hand moves the latter immediately. We advise the angler who is using a long line, and raising but not hooking a number of trout, to shorten his line, and he will at once be struck with the difference. We have invariably found that the nearer we are to our flies the better we can use them, and the greater is our chance of hooking a trout when it rises.

The advantages of the second part of the maxim to throw a light line it is impossible to over-estimate. The moment the flies light—being the only one in which trout take the artificial fly for a live one—is the most deadly in the whole cast, and consequently it is of immense importance to make the flies light in a soft and natural manner. To accomplish this, and to throw with certainty to any spot wished, requires great practice, and even the most practised angler can never make his flies fall so softly as an insect with outspread gauzy wings.

Thin gut, the necessity of which we have advocated so strongly, is exceedingly difficult to cast, as it has little weight to carry it forward, and therefore beginners should use moderately strong gut at first, and as they improve in casting reduce its size.

A difference of opinion exists as to whether a trout should be struck on rising; but in common with the great majority of anglers, we advocate immediate striking. When a trout takes a fly it shuts its mouth, and if the angler strikes then, he is almost sure to bring the hook into contact with its closed jaws. We have frequently watched the motions of trout on taking a fly, and when left to do with it what they choose, they very quickly expelled it from their mouths with considerable force; and we think that if the angler strikes even when the trout's mouth is open, he will have much better chance than by leaving it to hook itself. A trout on seizing an artificial fly is almost instantaneously aware that it is counterfeit, and never attempts to swallow it, very frequently letting it go before the angler has time to strike; so that it is of the utmost importance to strike immediately, and this is the reason why a quick eye and a ready hand are considered the most necessary qualifications for a fly-fisher. A trout first takes a fly, and then makes the motion which anglers term a rise, and which consists of their turning to go down; the angler therefore does not see the least break on the surface until the trout has either seized or missed the fly, so that he has already lost so much time, and should strike immediately.

Although it is impossible to strike too soon, it is quite possible to strike too hard. Some anglers strike with such force as to pull the trout out of the water, and throw it a considerable distance behind them. Now this is much too hard, and very apt with a small hook to tear it away from its hold, should it have any. Striking should be done by a slight but quick motion of the wrist, not by any motion of the arm. The angler should also take care to strike in the same direction as his rod is moving in at the time, for if he raises his rod, or otherwise alters its direction, the effect will not be nearly so immediate, and a moment is of the utmost importance in this matter.

One advantage of striking is, that should the trout miss the fly it rises at, the angler has still a chance of coming across it with some of the remaining ones. In a day's fishing we have frequently killed half a dozen trout hooked by the sides and other parts. And a trout hooked in this way always runs twice as hard as one hooked in the mouth. When hooked in the mouth, the strain that is kept on it prevents it from moving its gills, and suffocation ensues. This takes place sooner when the trout is drawn down a strong stream; so that the popular notion of pulling a trout down the water to drown it is correct, though the word is rather misapplied. If the trout is hooked by the outside of the body, the respiratory organs are left free, enabling it to run a long time; and when it does come to the side, the angler is disappointed at the small size of a fish which has been making such a desperate struggle.

In fishing up, the rise of a trout is by no means so distinct as in fishing down. They frequently seize the fly without breaking the surface, and the first intimation the angler gets of their presence is a slight pull at the line. The utmost attention is therefore necessary to strike the moment the least motion is either seen or felt. This is in some measure owing to the flies being in general a little under water, but principally to the fact that trout take a fly coming down stream in a quieter and more deadly manner than a fly going up. Seeing it going across and up stream, they seem afraid it may escape, make a rush at it, and in their hurry to seize, very frequently miss it altogether. It is very different in angling up stream: the trout see the fly coming towards them, rise to meet it, and seize it without any dash, but in a firm deadly manner.

When you hook a trout, if it is a small one and you are not wading, pull it on shore at once; if you are wading, it is better to act upon the maxim that "a bird in the hand is worth two in the bush," and come on shore before taking it off the hook, as it is very dangerous doing so when in the water. When you hook a large trout, which you cannot pull on shore at once, but require to exhaust previously, pull it down stream, as, in addition to choking it sooner, you have the force of the current in your favour. In playing a trout, do so as much as possible by keeping up with it by walking, and never let out line if you can avoid it. It is obvious that with a long line you cannot have the same command over it as with a short one; and take care never to allow your line to get slack, as, if you do, and the hook is not fixed, but merely resting on some bone, a thing which frequently occurs, the trout will throw it out of its mouth. To leave this point, in taking the trout out of the water do so with your hands, if you have not a landing-net; and never attempt lifting it by the line, or you are almost certain to pay dearly for your experience.

When you are approaching a pool which you intend to fish, if the water is clear do so carefully; you must recollect that the trout see you much more readily if you are on a high bank than if you are on a level with the water. For this reason keep as low down as possible, and always, if the nature of the ground will admit of it, stand a few yards from the edge of the water. If there is a ripple on the water you may meet with good sport in the still water at the foot of the pools, but if there is no wind, it is useless commencing till you come to where the water is agitated. If you do not intend fishing the lower part, do not walk up the side of it, as by so doing you will alarm the trout in that portion, and they may run up to the head of the pool for shelter, and frighten the others; but always come to the edge of the pool at the place where you intend to begin fishing. If the water is very low and the sun bright, it may be advisable to kneel in fishing a pool, in order to keep out of sight, and you must avoid allowing your shadow to fall upon the water above where you are standing.

First, as you approach, fish the side on which you are standing with a cast or two, and then commence to fish the opposite side, where you are to expect the most sport. For this reason you should always keep on the shallow side of the water, as the best trout generally lie under the bank at the deep side. After having taken a cast or two on the near side, throw your flies partly up stream and partly across, but more across than up, from where you are standing. You should throw them to within an inch of the opposite bank; if they alight on it so much the better; draw them gently off, and they will fall like a snow-flake, and if there is a trout within sight they are almost sure to captivate it. In this way your flies will fall more like a natural insect than by any other method.

After your flies alight, allow them to float gently down stream for a yard or two, taking care that neither they nor the line ripple the surface. There is no occasion for keeping them on the surface, they will be quite as attractive a few inches under water. As the flies come down stream, raise the point of your rod, so as to keep your line straight, and as little of it in the water as possible; and when they have traversed a few yards of water, throw again about a yard or two higher up than where your flies alighted the previous cast, and so on. Unless the spot looks exceedingly promising, you need not cast twice in one place if you do not get a rise, but if there is any quick turn in the water where there is likely to be a good trout, we frequently cast over it six or seven times in succession, just allowing the flies to alight when we cast again. Where the current is strong, the trout may not see the fly at first, and so we cast repeatedly to make sure; and we have frequently, after casting unsuccessfully half-a-dozen times over the same place, caught a good trout at last. Move up the pool as quickly as you can, first taking a cast or two straight up on the side you are on, and then fishing the opposite side, and so on, until you finish the pool. Although it is about the edges of the pool you will generally get most trout, the main current must by no means be neglected; indeed in it you will frequently capture the best fish. By fishing in the way we have described, throwing a yard or two further up every cast, the flies may be brought in a wonderfully short space of time over every foot of water where a trout is likely to be.

Streams should be fished in exactly the same manner as pools; fishing the side you are on straight up, and the opposite side partly across and partly up. All quiet water between two streams, and eddies behind stones, should be fished straight up, and the flies just allowed to remain sufficiently long to let the trout see them; and in fishing such places, care must be taken to keep the line out of the current. It is more difficult fishing streams than pools, as it requires greater nicety in casting; and on account of the roughness of the water it is not so easy to see a trout rise.

In fishing still water with no breeze upon it you should wait until the motion of the line falling has subsided, and then draw the flies slowly towards you, as, if they were allowed to remain stationary, the trout would at once detect their artificial nature.

Casting partly across and partly up stream, for a variety of reasons, is more deadly than casting directly up. The advantage of having a number of flies is entirely lost by casting straight up, as they all come down in a line, and it is only the trout in that line that can see them; whereas, if thrown partly across, they all come down in different lines, and the trout in all these lines may see them. In casting across, when the flies light, the stream carries them out at right angles to the line, and they come down the stream first, so that the trout sees the flies before the line; whereas, in casting straight up, if a trout is between the angler and the place where his flies light, the line passes over it before it sees the flies and may alarm it.

The moment the fly alights, being the most deadly of the whole cast, it is obvious that the oftener it is repeated the better, and therefore the angler should cast as frequently as possible, always allowing the flies to remain a few moments, in order to let the trout see them; but there is not much danger of casting too often, or even casting often enough, as the angler's arm will quickly rebel against it.

Rivers which can be commanded from bank to bank, either by wading or otherwise, constitute by far the most agreeable fishing; but if the river is so large that you cannot reach the opposite side, you must look for sport on the side you are on. And in this case, though you should neglect no spot where a trout may be lying, fish most carefully the part of the pool where the shallow merges into the deep, and where the current is moderately strong; fishing it in the same manner as you would do the opposite side, and always as you go up taking a cast or two straight up, as close to the edge as possible.

On all occasions cast your flies about a yard above where you think the trout are likely to be found, as if on alighting it attracts their attention, there is much less chance of their discovering its artificial nature at that distance. For the same reason, if you see a trout rise at a natural fly throw above it, and in general it will meet the fly half-way. If a trout rise and you miss it, cast again, and continue doing so until it ceases to rise; a small trout will frequently rise four or five times in succession; but the large well-conditioned fish are more wary, and if they miss once or twice will sometimes decline returning, however temptingly you may throw your flies.

A breezy day is generally considered favourable for fly-fishing, and no doubt it is so if the wind is blowing up stream; but it is equally likely that it may be blowing down—it generally blows either up or down, very seldom across—in which case the angler would be very much better without it. Because the wind is blowing down, the angler should on no account fish in the same direction, but must endeavour to cast against it as well as he can. He may, however, stand a little farther back from the water, and fish more nearly opposite to where he is standing than would otherwise be advisable. To cast against the wind, it is necessary to use great force, and immerse a considerable portion of the line in the water. If the wind is very strong, it is a great nuisance, no matter which way it is blowing, as it is sometimes almost impossible to keep the line in the water. In such circumstances it is impossible to fish the streams properly, and the angler should limit his operations to the pools, and should use thicker gut and a heavier casting-line, which will be found a great assistance to casting. It is in such a case that the thorough worthlessness of a supple rod becomes apparent.

As the trout seldom take fly readily for more than four or five hours in the forenoon, you must make the most of the time, fish quickly, walk over the intervening ground smartly, take the trout off the hook, and basket them as speedily as possible, and in every way economise time. If you ever see a professional angler at work when the trout are taking, watch him, and you will be able to form some idea of how expeditiously fishing may be done. As long as you are fishing, do it as if you expected a rise every cast; we have lost many a good trout in an inadvertent moment. If you are tired, or the trout are not taking, sit down and console yourself in some way or other. A late writer upon the subject suggests, that for this purpose the angler should carry a New Testament in his pocket, to which there can be no possible objection, but we rather think most anglers prefer spiritual consolation of a very different sort, coupled with sandwiches; there is a time for all things, and at noon we must admit having a preference for the latter method. It has moreover this advantage, that you will be the more able to fish properly when the trout begin to take again.

We have as yet said nothing about the adaptation of flies in point of size to the season of the year and the state of the water, because this subject is so intimately connected with the habits of the trout during the different fly-fishing months, that it is impossible to separate them, and we shall therefore discuss them together; but before commencing, we may remark, that a knowledge of the habits of the trout is the most necessary of all information to the angler. He may have the best tackle and the best flies, and be skilled in the art of throwing them lightly; but unless he knows where feeding trout are to be found, he will never achieve great success.

The two great causes which should regulate the angler in selecting the size of fly to be used are the colour and size of the water, and the wariness of the trout; the fly, in fact, *must be large enough to ensure its being seen, but not so large as to enable the trout to detect its artificial character.* When a river is large and dark-coloured, flies may be used a size or two larger than when it is clear; as in such circumstances it requires larger flies in order

SIZES OF FLY.

to be seen, and the thickness of the water prevents trout from detecting their artificial nature, as they would if the water was clear. In a dark windy day, a size or two larger may be used than in a calm sunny one, as the roughness of the water and the darkness of the sky prevent trout from seeing the flies so distinctly; therefore, the clearer the water and brighter the day, the smaller should the fly be, and the thicker the water and darker the day, the larger should it be; always increasing or diminishing the fly as circumstances prevent its being easily seen, or the reverse.

Where trout are not much fished for, larger flies may be used than where the reverse is the case, as the trout under these circumstances get suspicious, and look twice at a fly before they take it. The reason why shy trout will take a small fly more readily than a large one is, that since they cannot see it so distinctly, its artificial nature is not so easily detected. In streams where the trout are very shy we generally find that the very smallest fly raises most fish.

When commencing a day's fly-fishing at any season, the angler should begin with three or four different varieties—say a black spider for the tail-fly, a woodcock wing with yellow silk and red hackle for the first dropper, a hare-lug body and corn-bunting wing for the second dropper, and a dun-coloured spider for the fourth fly. It will be found advisable, if the trout evince a decided preference for any of them, to put on two or three of that sort, leaving on one of a different colour in case of any change in the humour of the fish, which, however, rarely happens. We have invariably found ourselves gainers by adopting this method, and that the droppers which had before been doing little killed their due proportion when changed to the taking fly.

In order to ascertain the relative value of the tail-fly and the droppers, we fished for a succession of days with three flies of exactly the same size, colour, and shape, and tied upon gut of the same thickness. At the conclusion, the proportion stood 3, 2, 2, the droppers thus capturing the same number, and the tail-fly a half more than either of them. We also fished for several days with four flies of the same kind, when the proportion was 12, 7, 6, 8. The tail-fly has the best chance, because in casting to the opposite bank, where the most trout are taken with the fly, it alone reaches it. The gut is also only on one side of it, whereas the others have gut on both sides. It will be seen that after the tail-fly, the dropper nearest the line has the next best chance, which we ascribe to its being nearest the bank when casting on the same side of the water on which we were standing. The foregoing trials were made with the view of ascertaining when a fly is not doing its duty and ought to be changed; they were all conducted in a river which could be commanded from bank to bank. In a large river we should suppose that the proportions would be slightly different, and that the tail-fly would not kill so much in proportion.

The time of year when trout begin to take fly readily entirely depends upon the nature of the river and the season. They never rise freely at the artificial fly until they are accustomed to feed upon the natural insect; and the first insects which make their appearance in any quantity are the March browns. It is not until these flies have been a week or ten days on the water, or at a time, varying according to the season and district from the middle to the end of April, that fly-fishing really commences. In that short space of time trout improve wonderfully in condition, and leaving the still water, where they have had their haunts during winter, move up into the stronger parts of the pools, about the sides of which they lie in wait for their prey.

If the weather is mild, which it rarely is at this season of east winds, the end of April is the best fly-fishing time of the whole season. The trout take with a readiness and certainty which they never exhibit at any subsequent period. Flies are still a rarity to them, and they are not yet shy from being over-fed, or from a frequent view or more practical experience of artificial flies. Other reasons why more trout can be captured with the fly at this season than any other are, that there are more trout in the water—the summer's fishing and netting not having begun yet—and that the trout are more concentrated in particular places.

As regards the imitation of the March brown, which is held in such high estimation amongst anglers, if the water is heavy, trout will sometimes take it readily, not because they see any resemblance between it and the real March brown—at least we never could—but because it is a good size of fly for the season; any of the flies we have mentioned, dressed of the same size, will be equally killing. The flies used this month should in general be full size; if the waters are coloured, Nos. 9 and 10 will be found most effective; but if the waters are small, a size or two less will be advisable.

At this season a warm sunny day is most favourable to the angler. The birth of flies depends in a great measure upon the state of the weather; and when there are no natural flies on the water, trout never rise freely at an artificial one. An east wind or a cold frosty day is a death-blow to the angler's hopes, as in such there are no flies to be seen, and the trout retire to deep water. In this month we have frequently seen, about eleven o'clock in the forenoon, a perfect shower of March browns come on the water, which for half-an-hour or so appeared almost boiling with trout leaping; and then the flies went off and all was quiet again. Till the flies appeared we met with no sport;

when they were on the water we got a rise almost every cast, and when they went away we hardly got another trout.

This is what is popularly known as "the time of the take," and occurs more or less, at some time of the day, the whole season through. The leaping of the trout in all directions at once informs the angler when it commences, and he should make the most of his time. It sometimes happens several times during the day, but rarely lasts more than an hour at a time, and stops as suddenly as it commences. It is only during the take that a trout can be caught in very deep water, as it is only then they are hovering near the surface on the outlook for flies. Once it is over they retire to the bottom and there lie; and if the water is very deep they may not be able to see the angler's flies, or if they do, cannot be troubled to rise and seize them; so that when trout are not taking freely, the angler will always meet with most success in comparatively shallow water.

In April the angler must look for sport in the pools, as the trout are not yet strong enough to lie in the streams, and therefore it is of no use fishing in them. There are some parts of a pool in which trout are, at all seasons, more likely to be found than in others. There are always plenty of them lying in the shallow water at the pool-foot, which, if there is a ripple on it, will be found the best place of all. Passing up to the deeper portions of the pool, the trout are more congregated about the sides, as it is there that the aquatic insects on which they feed are most numerous. They choose convenient feeding stations below some large stone or tuft of grass, where the river runs beneath the bank, or where a projecting bush affords food and shelter to some finny giant who holds his revels below. Such places are always sure to be tenanted, and what is rather singular, the best feeding station in a pool or stream is generally occupied by the largest trout in it, and if it is captured the next largest takes its place; and we have day after day caught a trout in one spot, each capture being of smaller dimensions than its predecessor.

In cold weather, in the early part of the season, we have generally found the sunny side of the water the best; we suppose because there are more insects there.

Passing from April to May, trout improve greatly in condition, and move into stronger water about the heads of pools, scattering themselves, but not plentifully as yet, through the streams. Of all places where the angler is likely to find trout at any season, the meeting of two streams is the best; there, in the quiet water between and on either side of the strong runs, feeding trout are sure to be lying watching to seize whatever the stream brings in the way of food. Such places should always be fished with great care.

For fishing slow-running streams, the end of

April and beginning of May are the best times, and the trout in such are then in excellent condition; but for rivers in general, the month of May, taking it as a whole, is worth any two months to the fly-fisher. Sport may be more relied upon than in the preceding month. The birth and appearance of flies on the water is rendered less dependent on the weather; a cold day or an east wind does not do the same mischief, and the trout will generally take during the whole day, unless the weather is extremely cold. We have never at this season found it of any use to attempt fly-fishing before seven or eight in the morning; the forenoon, from eight till about noon or an hour or two after, we consider the best time; about two they generally leave off taking, but commence again in the evening, if the weather is mild. In the beginning of the month we have generally met with more success in a warm sunny day; but to tell the most favourable weather with anything like certainty is impossible, as the trout are very capricious, and will sometimes take readily during a hail-storm, while at other times, in such a case, not a trout will rise. Towards the end of the month we prefer a showery day with west wind, or a thoroughly wet one if the weather is warm.

The best condition of water for capturing trout is when there is just sufficient rain to raise the water slightly, and make it of an amber colour. When a large flood occurs, it scatters the trout too much, and they become gorged with food, and do not take so readily; so that more trout can generally be caught in clear water than after a heavy flood. If the water is only coloured or slightly swollen, trout will be found in the same places as when it is clear; but when the water is large and dark-coloured, it is of no use fishing the streams, as they are too rapid, and in the pools the trout are all congregated about the sides. In such circumstances, therefore, the angler should not waste time fishing the centre of the pool, but merely fish the sides; fishing the side he is on straight up and as close to the edge as possible, and the opposite side partly across and partly up as usual. The greatest number will frequently be got on the thin side, but the largest and best trout are almost invariably caught on the deep side, and very close to the edge.

The flies used in May should be smaller than those used in April; if the waters are clear, No. 11 or 12 will answer very well, but if the rivers are coloured, a size larger may be used; a good-sized fly will frequently catch the best trout in heavy water.

Towards the end of this month the stone-fly, or May-fly of Tweedside, makes its appearance— the green drake, to which the name of May-fly is usually applied, not appearing for a fortnight later. These flies give the first great blow to artificial fly-fishing; they are so large, and the trout get them in such abundance, that before they have been many days on the water, the trout become quite satiated with surface food. They are now in prime condition—strong and vigorous—affording excellent play when hooked. They also forsake the deeper portions of the pools, moving up into the strong water at the head, and into broken water and streams, where they choose convenient feeding stations, such as eddies behind stones, below banks, and submersed tufts of grass, and, in short, every place where they can remain unseen, and watch for their prey as it comes down stream towards them; and the angler should neglect no place where he thinks there is a trout.

About this time they begin to act the epicure, becoming exceedingly nice in their tastes, and paying little attention to the angler's lure, and they may frequently be seen following, without making any attempt to seize it. When they are in this mood, which generally lasts till the beginning of August, always use spiders, and reduce their size to No. 12 or 13; a No. 14 midge may also be used with advantage. This, to a certain extent, meets their views, it being more suspicion of the nature of the fly than want of inclination to seize it, which makes them so nice. On such occasions, also, the angler should pass over the pools, and fish the streams, as in them, owing to the roughness of the water, the trout cannot so easily detect the artificial nature of the flies.

From the middle of June to the beginning of

August is the worst part of the whole season for fly-fishing. In large rivers, such as Tweed, and all slow-running streams, fly-fishing—at least during the day—is not worth practising. At sunset, however, trout will rise freely, and continue to do so all night if the weather is favourable. A dry, warm night, with little dew falling, will generally be found most favourable; if there is much dew falling or a thick mist rising from the water—the surrounding country being free from it—trout will not take freely. At night they leave the streams and pool-heads, to cruise about among the pool-foots and shallows, and it is in these places that the angler should fish for them. Two flies will generally be found sufficient for night-fishing, and they should be a good deal larger than those used during the day. The largest trout caught during the summer months are usually taken at night, as it is only then that they leave the bottom of the deep pools in search of food.

At this season the fly-fisher, in search of sport during the day, should have recourse to the smaller waters and more backward districts of the country, where the trout are not yet—indeed in some places they never are—satiated with surface food. Fly-fishing at this season is more difficult than at any other; for, unless in a very favourable day, the trout will not rise in the pools; the **angler**, therefore, must have recourse to the streams and

NIGHT-FISHING.

rough broken water, and to fish these successfully with the fly is very nice practice indeed. The flies alone should touch the water, and they should never be thrown into the main current, but into nooks and eddies, and all those places where the worm-fisher would look for sport, and which will be indicated in a subsequent chapter. The trout that will take a worm will generally rise at a spider if thrown lightly over it; but in fly-fishing the angler cannot capture one-fourth of the trout that rise, whereas in worm-fishing he can make sure of one out of two offers, which accounts for the comparatively few trout in the fly-fisher's basket at this season.

In clear sunny days, trout may frequently be seen basking in shallow water, which, at first sight, seems scarcely sufficient to cover them. On such occasions they will rise greedily at a spider, if the angler keeps well out of sight, and throws lightly over them; he must also take care that the shadow of his rod does not fall upon the water in their neighbourhood. The capture of one will, however, scare away the others, and they will not return for some time.

Trout will rarely, even in the heat of summer, take fly readily early in the morning; they generally commence about six, and continue taking for four or five hours, when they stop for some time; commencing again in the evening, if the weather is favourable. At all seasons, the forenoon is the best time, unless, perhaps, in June and July, when they will take most freely about sunset.

The atmosphere at this season is frequently in a calm thundery state, with heavy white clouds floating about, which is not favourable to the angler. From the end of May to the end of August, a drizzling or thoroughly wet day is the best; next to which is a showery one, and then a bright day with a breeze of wind; a dark day without wind is the worst of all. East wind, which is looked upon with so much horror at the commencement of the season, is not at all objectionable now; being rather favourable than otherwise, as it is generally accompanied with a cool atmosphere.

In July we have always met with even less sport when the water was coloured than when it was clear, which we can only account for by supposing that as it is the worm season, the trout are on the outlook for this description of food, and pay no attention to the flies; at least in such circumstances we never see many rises at the natural insect.

In the summer months it is considered a great improvement to hook a maggot to the end of the fly, but this is not fly-fishing, and changes the character of the lure from the most clean and pleasant to the most disagreeable of all the methods of capturing trout. It has, moreover, at all times a substitute in a fine red worm, which is much more agreeable to handle, and will kill two for one which the fly with the maggot will.

August is a better month for the fly than July, and during the whole of it, but especially at the latter end, trout rise freely. Night-fishing may now be said to be at an end; the nights in general are cold and frosty, and the trout will not rise freely; so that there is little inducement to leave a comfortable bed to shiver at the waterside. By the beginning of September there is a visible change for the worse in the condition of the trout—they are full of spawn, and are fast losing strength, firmness, and flavour. They now commence to leave the streams, and return to the pools and more quiet water; it is worthy of remark, that those which remain in the streams are generally in good condition; if they were not, they would not have strength to keep their place in strong water. The flies used this month, as well as in the end of August, should be a size or two larger than those used during summer—approaching in size to a spring fly. After a flood, capital sport may be had; the trout will rise almost as freely as in the month of May, and though in general out of condition, the angler will still meet with some that will test freely both his skill and tackle. They will continue taking through October, but excepting the small ones, are in such poor condition as to be totally unfit for use.

The sizes of flies we have indicated are those

suitable for southern streams. In Highland rivers, where the trout are not so numerous or wary, flies considerably larger than those we have mentioned will frequently secure the best trout.

Fly-fishing in streams inhabited by cunning, cautious trout, when the water is low and clear, is undoubtedly the kind of fishing which requires most science. And for our own part we would rather capture ten pounds weight of trout in some much-fished southern stream open to the public, than twice that quantity in some preserved water, or remote Highland stream, where the trout seldom see an artificial fly, and are ready to seize anything that presents itself in the shape of food. Fishing in preserved water loses a great part of its pleasure. We like to be free to seek trout where we like, and take them where we can; and as there is more merit, there is more pleasure, in filling a basket where all anglers, high and low, rich and poor, are free to do the same, than in a river, fished only by a favoured few. All beginners in the art, if they wish to excel, should commence in streams where the trout are remarkably shy, and they will the sooner become skilful. If they commence in Highland streams, where the trout are half-starved, and where it requires little exercise or skill to capture them, they will get into a careless style of fishing, which they may find it difficult to alter. We have known anglers from the north, who considered themselves, and were considered, good fishers, and who in their own streams could kill seven or eight dozen trout in a day, unable to secure half-a-dozen small fish in our southern streams. The angler who can kill trout in streams such as Tweed, Gala, or Almond,* which are fished by dozens every day, may rest assured that he is quite able to kill them wherever they are to be found.

* Mr. Stewart here seems to allude to the Mid-Lothian and Linlithgowshire Almond, from which almost all fish life has now been driven by the paraffine works.

CHAPTER VII.

ON ANGLING WITH THE WORM.

FISHING with the worm is not usually held in such high estimation as it deserves; a circumstance entirely owing to its being but very imperfectly understood. Fly-fishers are apt to sneer at worm-fishing as a thing so simple that any one may succeed in it—their notions of it being that it is practised either when the waters are swollen after rain, or with a float and sinkers in some deep pool; and it is not surprising that with such ideas of it they should hold it in contempt. Worm-fishing is only worthy of the name of sport when practised in streams inhabited by wary trout, when they are low and clear. Under such circumstances it becomes a branch of the art, which, to be pursued with success, requires the most intimate acquaintance with the habits of the trout, and the nicest powers of casting; and which in point of difficulty is only inferior to fly-fishing. Those anglers who despise worm-fishing as a thing so simple as to be quite unworthy of their attention, would quickly discover their mistake if brought to a small clear water on a warm sunny day in June or July.

As a lure for trout, worm unquestionably ranks next to artificial fly. It also comes in at a very suitable time—being the very season in which the fly-fisher meets with least encouragement. One advantage it possesses over fly is the superior size of the trout caught; in general they will average a half more in weight. If any angler is limited to one week's fishing in the year, he should choose bright weather and clear water in the beginning of July; if skilled in the use of the worm, he may depend upon killing more trout then than any other week in the year.

The first subject which naturally suggests itself is the tackle necessary for this mode of fishing. The rod should be at least four feet longer than that used for fly.

A double-handed rod should be used on all occasions, and in all waters, whether small or large. A single-handed rod is most suitable for fly-fishing, where quick striking is necessary, and where a line several times the length of the rod can be thrown with ease ; but in worm-fishing, quick striking is not necessary, and throwing a long line is highly reprehensible, as the force required to cast it mutilates the worm sadly. For this reason also, the rod for worm-fishing should be rather more pliant, as it requires more force and a more sudden impulse to cast a certain length of line with a stiff rod than with a moderately supple one. As you cannot cast a long line, keeping out of the trout's sight must be managed by length of rod, not by length of line; and a single-handed rod can never accomplish this properly. The rod should not be shorter than from fourteen to sixteen feet. This, with a line from once to once and a half as long as the rod, is sufficient to keep the angler out of sight in the clearest water. The rods made in the fishing-tackle shops for bait-fishing are generally very well adapted for the purpose, and are not, like the fly-rods, made too supple.

The reel, line, and casting-line should be the same as those used for fly-fishing; and the hook should be joined to the latter by seven or eight lengths of picked gut. The gut used for this purpose, as well as for dressing the hooks on, should be the very finest that can be had. An opinion is quite current among anglers, that fine gut is by no means necessary for bait-fishing; and when assorting a hank, they lay aside the fine threads for fly, and the remainder for bait. This is a great mistake—fine gut being equally necessary for both methods. We once, on passing over a bridge, when returning from a day's fishing, observed a trout of about a pound weight basking in the sun, in water not half-a-foot deep. Wishing to ascertain if he was inclined to take a worm, we threw one in a little above him. This he devoured eagerly, as also another. We then baited our hook and threw it in above him; but on its approaching he made off very quickly, being evidently alarmed by the gut.

In dressing bait-hooks, take a well-waxed red silk thread, and commence by giving it a turn or two round the end of the shank of the hook, to prevent the latter from cutting the gut; then laying the gut to the hook, whip both firmly together rather more than half-way up the shank, where finish with a succession of hitch-knots or the whip-fastening.

With regard to the size of hook, we think a small size, not larger than No. 3 or 4, is best, being much more easily swallowed, and less likely to be discovered by the trout. When baiting, take the hook, and entering it close to the head end of the worm, run the worm up on it and on the gut, till it is all impaled but about three-quarters of an inch of the tail, which should be left to play about. The object of this is, that the trout, which always makes its first attack upon the part which appears most lively, may seize the end where the hook is. It is the practice of some anglers to leave a large part of the head to move about, under the supposition that the worm will live longer. This is very objectionable, as in such circumstances the trout may make its first attack on the head, and may be alarmed by getting the gut in its mouth; or the angler may strike before it takes hold of the hook at all, and consequently lose the trout.

With every precaution, however, the angler will sometimes miss three or four trout in succession, because they have not got the hook in their mouth, but merely bite some part of the worm. In such circumstances three or four small hooks about No. 9 or 10 of Bartlett's, or what are perhaps even better, three of Hutchinson and Son's sneck-bent hooks, No. 3 or 4, tied to one thread of gut, will be found much more effective than a single hook.

The accompanying illustration shows the tackle and the method of baiting it, which requires no explanation.

The advantages of this tackle are—that a trout can hardly take hold of the worm at all without having one of the hooks in its mouth; that the worm lives much longer, and being free to wriggle itself into any shape, is more natural-looking and consequently enticing; and lastly, that it is much more easily baited, particularly if the worms are fresh. Its disadvantages are—that it is more difficult to extricate from the trout's mouth; that it requires to be baited afresh every bite; and that the exposure of so many hooks is calculated to scare away some trout that would otherwise take the bait. But, upon the whole, the advantages preponderate considerably over the disadvantages, particularly when trout are biting shy.

From using this tackle occasionally and finding it answer, we were led to think that by using it continually more trout might be captured than with the common bait-hook. We resolved to devote three successive days in order to test this, and to fish one half hour with the common hook, and the next with three or four small ones; varying the number and size to suit the worms. The first trial was in Gala, between Bowland and Stow, where the trout are of good size and remarkably wary; so that the exposure of the hooks would tell with full force. On this occasion we captured $20\frac{1}{2}$ lbs. of trout, of which $9\frac{1}{2}$ lbs. were taken with the common hook and 11 lbs. with the tackle. The next trial was in Leader, between Earlston and Lauder, when we captured with the common hook $14\frac{1}{2}$ lbs., and with the tackle $17\frac{1}{2}$ lbs. The third day was also in Leader, when the result was with the common hook $12\frac{1}{2}$ lbs., and with the tackle $13\frac{1}{2}$ lbs.—making a total during the three days of $36\frac{1}{2}$ lbs. with the common hook, and 42 lbs. with the tackle; leaving a difference in favour of the latter of $5\frac{1}{2}$ lbs., or about fifteen per cent. Had we been fishing all these days with the single hook, we should only have had 19 lbs., 29 lbs., and 25 lbs. respectively; whereas, had we fished continually with the tackle, we should have had 22 lbs., 35 lbs., and 27 lbs.—no small difference. All these trials were made in the middle of July, when the waters were very small and clear, and consequently when every objection that can be urged against the four hooks was likely to tell with full force; added to which, the stones, as is frequently the case after long-continued dry weather, were covered with green slimy vegetable matter, which stuck to the small hooks whenever they came in contact with it, and occasioned considerable loss of time.

A brother of the writer made the same trial with the same result. He also observed that with the tackle he got fewer trout, but larger ones, which seems surprising, but may be accounted for by supposing that though some trout had been alarmed by the exposure of the hooks, the lively and natural appearance of the worm had been more attractive to large trout. Whether or not every angler will meet with the same result, *entirely depends upon his capabilities for baiting and managing the respective tackles;* but probably all really good anglers will catch more weight of trout with the three or four small hooks than with the one large one; and since we first introduced it to the attention of anglers

SINKERS.

four years ago, it has come into very general use.

Whatever kind of hooks the angler is using, he should pay great attention to the state of his worm, and if it has become maimed or waterlogged, change it, as a lively worm is more enticing than a dead one.

Split shot to regulate the rate of the worm down stream are usually considered indispensable by the angler; but, except on rare occasions, impeding the motion of the worm is objectionable, and for the following reasons:—A worm thrown into a stream would be carried down by the current and turned round in every eddy; and as this is the way in which trout are accustomed to see worms coming down stream, every deviation from it is calculated to excite their suspicion. When there are two or three split shot on the line, the worm travels at a slower rate than the stream, and yields but little to any eddy. The shot control and retard its movements, so that, looking upon the shot as almost stationary, the line between them and the worm, and of course the worm itself at the end of it, are dangling about in the stream; in fact, to a certain extent, resisting the current, instead of being carried down by it. Again, if the worm is thrown into an eddy, the shot go to the bottom and lie there; but the worm, being much lighter, rises with the current as far as the length of line between it and the shot, and there remains almost stationary. Now, in both these cases, the shot give an unnatural motion to the worm.

The alleged advantages of shotting are, that the worm travels more slowly, affording the trout plenty of time to seize it, and that it always reaches the bottom. Now, as to the first assertion, the best rate for the worm to travel at is undoubtedly the natural one, and if the trout wish to seize it, they have always plenty of time to do so. To the second reason we attach some importance; it is natural for the worm to be near the bottom, and with sinkers the angler will certainly catch trout in deeper water than he could without them, but as a rule it is not in deep water that the worm-fisher must look for sport; and in water not above a couple of feet deep, the worm will reach the bottom very quickly without any assistance; and even should it not, the trout will rise to seize it, frequently jumping at it as they would at a fly. The only occasions in which the use of sinkers can be defended are, either when the wind is blowing so strong that it would be impossible to keep the line in the water without them, or when it is necessary to fish water so deep that the trout would not see the worm unless they were used.

Besides giving an unnatural motion to the worm, sinkers are highly objectionable in other respects. They are constantly hanking below stones, and occasioning the angler a great deal of annoyance and loss of time. With them also the angler gets over the ground at a much slower rate than when his worm comes down almost at the same rate as the stream. This opinion about sinkers is held by almost all the best worm-fishers; and some Tweedside adepts never use them under any circumstances.

Many different kinds of worms are used by the angler, but the four following are held in highest estimation, and are also to be found in greatest abundance. In Edinburgh they may be had ready for use at a very moderate price; but in country places the angler will frequently require to dig and prepare his own bait, or he will be but indifferently provided, and therefore it behoves him to know the places where he may find them, and how to prepare them.

THE BLACK-HEADED WORM. — This worm is usually found in good garden soil, or among heaps of decayed rubbish, and may be known by being free from the knot which most worms have. As its name signifies, it has a black head, and when taken from the earth is of a darkish colour throughout, which it loses when scoured, becoming of a clear reddish tinge, and is a very inviting worm to look at. As an angling bait it deserves the first rank, being the most durable of all worms. The only objections to it are—the length of time it takes to scour, and the difficulty of getting any number of a proper size.

THE BRANDLING is only to be found in an old dunghill or similar place, and it may be known by being ringed all round, with a knot a little above the middle: it is also flatter in shape than most worms. We hold this worm in great repute; it can be scoured in a day or two, and is then a beautiful worm to appearance. It is also in general of the very size the angler would wish. The principal objection to brandlings is their extreme softness; they are incapable of being toughened, and when used upon a single hook, slip down upon the bend, thus exposing the shank. This objection does not apply to them when used upon the four small hooks, and we very often use them in this way. When pierced they emit a very offensive smell, but anglers must not be too particular in this respect.

THE MARSH WORM.—When taken from the earth this worm is of a pale-blue colour, with a whitish knot a little above the centre. It is a very small worm, and is more usually found too small than too large. If kept sufficiently long it becomes of a lively pink colour, and may be used with great success, particularly in small waters. It is the most plentiful of all descriptions of worms, and may be found in any garden among heaps of decayed rubbish and below stones.

THE RED-HEADED WORM.—This worm is only to be found plentifully in the very richest soil, about the edges of dunghills and similar places.

SIZE OF WORM.

It is of a dark-red colour on the head and all down the back, and of a pale-blue colour underneath. As a bait for trout it does not deserve much attention. It is so thick in proportion to its length, that if it is sufficiently long to cover the hook, it makes too large a bait, and after it has been a very short time in the water it loses its colour, becoming quite dark, and consequently not so attractive.

With regard to the size of worm for fishing where the trout are well fed and wary when the waters are clear, worms can hardly be used too small if they cover the hook. A worm from two to three inches long, and about the thickness of a hen's quill, is the largest size that should be used. A small bright clean worm is always most enticing to well-fed trout; and it is quite common to meet anglers using worms so large as effectually to prevent their having the least sport. It is a great error to suppose that a large worm insures a large trout; quite the reverse. A large worm will seldom capture anything but some audacious little fellow of a parr, or equally insignificant trout.

Trout do not seem to evince any decided preference for one kind of worm before another, so that the angler may use whichever kind he likes best or can get most easily. The great point is to have them of the right size and well scoured. When newly dug, they are so full of earth as to be unfit for use. Brandlings may be scoured in a day or two; but the other kinds require to be kept at least a week. Immediately on being dug, they should be washed in water, and put into an earthenware jar with plenty of moss. The moss should be well washed, and rung as hard as possible, and all the small sticks and straws picked carefully out, as they are apt to cut the worms. The jar should be examined every second or third day, and all the dead or sickly worms picked out and the moss changed. The process of toughening worms can only be accomplished by keeping the moss dry, so that the worms may lose some of the moisture of their bodies, and thus become tougher and more durable. This is objectionable, as it impairs the vitality of the worms, giving them, if carried to any extent, a very withered look. When thoroughly divested of earthy matter, worms can be easily baited; and they will last quite long enough without going through the additional process of toughening, or rather drying. The worm-jar should always be kept in a cool place.

For containing worms when angling, a flannel bag, large enough to admit the hand freely, will be found the most convenient receptacle. It should have a loop attached to it, by which it may be fastened to the button of the angler's coat, and a separate string to tie round the mouth. If the angler intends fishing long at a time, he will find it an improvement to divide his worms, keeping one-half in a bag in his basket till required. The repeated thrusting in of the angler's hand, the dangling of the bag, and exposure to the sun, will greatly injure the worms before the day is out, if the whole supply is kept in one bag.

The angler should be very particular about the size and appearance of his worms, and should never start for a day's trouting without a sufficient supply. Nothing is more provoking than to run short of bait at the very time the trout are taking. Under any circumstances, a gross and a half or two gross is the smallest number that should be taken for a day's trouting with worm.

Worm-fishing is better understood than fly-fishing; that is to say, there are more anglers who fish up stream with the one than with the other. Angling up stream with the worm possesses all the advantages which have been mentioned in fly-fishing, and which it is unnecessary to recapitulate. The objections against fishing down stream apply with even greater force to worm-fishing than to fly, as in fly-fishing the angler can keep out of sight, to a certain extent, by throwing a long line. Not so in worm-fishing; he must either be opposite or below his worm, so that every trout in the neighbourhood of his line can see him distinctly; and if he were to fish down a small clear water with the worm, he would hardly catch a trout, while his neighbour fishing up stream might fill his basket. All worm-fishers of the present day that know anything about the matter invariably throw their worm up stream.

In trouting with the worm, a proper casting of the line is of great importance. The two things to be attended to are, to throw lightly, so as not to break the worm, and to throw with certainty to any required spot. To accomplish the first mentioned, some recommend heaving or pitching the line forward; but this is a very uncertain method, quite impracticable in a windy day, and hardly practicable at any time, unless there is plenty of shot on the line. We do not see that it mutilates the worm less than the ordinary method; and at best the line can never be thrown with the same certainty.

In casting a worm, you should allow it to go out behind, and then urge it forward slowly; all sudden jerks must be avoided, as they are apt to tear the worm, and force it down on the bend of the hook, thus exposing the shank. You must also allow the point of your rod to go nearer the water than in casting a fly, as it is necessary to extend the rod to the full length, in order to get the bait as far out as possible. In doing this, you must not lower the point of your rod till you have given the worm all the forward impetus you intend; then lower it slowly almost to a level with the water, and the worm will go to the full stretch of both rod and line. Whenever the worm lights, raise your rod gradually, so as to keep as little of your

OF KEEPING LITTLE LINE IN WATER.

line in the water as possible; but you must take care not to raise it so quickly as in any way to interfere with the motion of the worm. It is of great importance that there should be very little line in the water, not so much because it is calculated to alarm the trout, as because the action of the stream upon the line will in some cases bring the worm down much faster than it would otherwise come, and in others bring it nearer the surface. If you throw your worm into an eddy or any quiet piece of water at the side of a stream, and any part of the line alights in the current, the worm will be swept out almost instantaneously. When you throw your worm and line into an open stream, the worm presenting considerable surface to its action is carried down almost at the same rate as the stream; but the line, not presenting so much surface to the action of the water, lags behind. If this takes place to any extent, and there is much line farther up the stream than the worm, the stream still pressing on the worm, and the line above presenting some resistance to the free progress of the worm down stream, it is brought nearer the surface. To avoid this, the angler should keep his rod a little farther down stream than his worm, and should have no part of his line in the water, but four or five feet of the very finest gut, which should now and then be drawn gently down stream, so as to keep as little line above the worm as possible. It is by attending to this that the angler can keep his worm near the bottom; but it must be done so gently that it will neither pull the worm down stream nor nearer the surface. If this be properly done, the angler will catch a half more trout than if he were keeping a large quantity of line immersed in the water. For the length of line, the angler will be guided entirely by circumstances; but it will rarely be found necessary to use one much longer than the rod.

The first notice you get of a trout's having taken your bait is in general a stoppage of the line. This, however, may arise from the hook or line having come in contact with some fixed object. You should therefore lower the point of your rod down stream till your line is straight, when you will at once know whether or not there is a trout at it. The proper time to strike depends upon whether you are using a common bait-hook or the four-hook tackle. If you are using the latter, strike down stream as soon as you can get your line straight. If you are using a common bait-hook, it is difficult to know the proper time to strike. You may strike before the trout has the hook in its mouth at all, or you may give it so long that it may discover the hook and expel it from its mouth. In either case you lose the trout. A trout, when taking a worm, frequently seizes the part that is up on the line and quite free from the hooks, and will carry it away to his lair before attempting to swallow it. A pull at the line intimates that a trout has taken the

METHOD OF FISHING POOLS. 151

worm; there is then generally an even pull and running out of the line; and when this stops, which indicates that the trout has arrived at his starting-place, the angler should strike, and in general he will secure the trout.

You will frequently observe, when you have caught a trout, or even had one on for a moment, that the worm is off the hooks and a considerable distance up the line, sometimes past one or even two knots. This shows that trout must possess some extraordinary power of expelling from their mouths what they find disagreeable, as it is certainly the fish that does it, and not the dangling of the line, or any motion of the stream or rod.

In fishing pools, if the water is very clear and low, approach carefully. In general, it will be found advisable to kneel; and, as in fly-fishing, you should come to the water-side at the place where you intend commencing, and should also keep on the shallow side of the water. With a line a little longer than your rod, throw your worm gently as far up from you as possible, and allow it to come down nearly opposite to where you are standing, when you should throw again. Casting partly across and partly up is more deadly than casting directly up; the reason of which is, that in casting directly up, if there is a trout between the angler and the place where the worm lights, all the line passes over it before it sees the bait, and may alarm it. Two casts in one place will in general be sufficient to determine if there is any trout inclined to take; but if you get a bite, you should of course cast there again.

In fishing streams, cast in the same direction as in fishing pools; but as the water is rougher, you will not be so easily seen, and kneeling is unnecessary. You should always throw your worm a few yards above where you think a trout is lying, as by the time the bait reaches it, it will be pretty well sunk, and trout take a worm most readily near the bottom. As you will invariably get most trout on the opposite side of the water from where you are standing, always keep on the side where you think there are fewest trout lying. The practice adopted by some anglers of wading up the centre of the stream, and casting on both sides of them, answers very well in large rivers, where there is plenty of water to conceal the angler; but in small rivers it alarms the trout. Not that the trout, where the angler casts his line, sees him; but those about the part of the water where he is standing run up and alarm the others. The better plan is to fish the side you are on as you approach, and then, if necessary, wade in to fish the opposite. But on all occasions, make as little disturbance and keep as little line in the water as possible.

With regard to the season when worm-fishing commences, a few trout may be taken with the worm in April and May; but at this season there is no inducement to use it, as trout take fly much more readily; and if the angler must have a bait, he will find a much more deadly one in the May-fly, which forms the subject of the next chapter. There are some anglers who never fish with anything else but worms; a proceeding we can only account for by supposing that they are deficient both in knowledge and taste. When worm-fishing is not in season, the trout captured by it are neither so large or so well-conditioned as those taken with the fly. Trout never take a worm freely till they are thoroughly satiated with surface food; and this seldom happens until the May-flies are off the water, or at a time varying from the beginning of June to the beginning of July. It is now that worm-fishing commences in earnest, and really good and exciting sport it is. The trout are in splendid condition, strong and vigorous; so that a half-pound trout at this season will afford as much play as one of twice the size would have done two months earlier. It is the most certain and deadly of all fishing; and by it more trout may be captured in the month of July than by any other means in any other month of the year. And he is not worthy of the name of angler who cannot, in any day of the month, when the water is clear, kill from fifteen to twenty pounds weight of trout in any county in the south of Scotland.*

Sport can also be more relied upon in this than in any other kind of angling; thunder in the air,

---

* See introductory chapter, and footnote.

that dread of the fly-fisher, does little harm here. We never found trout taking better than one day in Gala during a thunder-storm, when we captured $22\frac{1}{2}$ lbs. of trout, and they continued taking as readily as ever, till about one o'clock, when suddenly the water, which before had been clear, came down quite thick and muddy, and put an end to further sport.

The first part of the day is undoubtedly the best, and the angler should arrange so as to have the bulk of his take by twelve o'clock; but if the day is dark and the sun comes out about four P.M., or a mild shower falls, very good sport may be had up to a late hour in the evening. If the weather is favourable, the angler cannot commence too early; trout will take readily when there is only sufficient light to bait a hook. A dry morning, with little dew, or a rainy one, if it is warm, will generally be found best; but if there is much dew falling, or a thick mist rising from the waters, trout will not take till some time after the sun is up. Early in the morning—that is to say, before six or seven o'clock—trout will take worm readily in the streamy portions of the pools, in water where there is not much chance of success during the day. Numbers of trout, which have been cruising about the shallows all night, have not yet returned to the streams, but are lying in the strong deep water. Morning fishing, however, is very uncertain, and seven o'clock is quite early enough to start.

PLACES WHERE TO FISH.

If trout have been taking readily in the early part of the morning, a lull usually takes place for an hour or so, about six or seven; and if they have not been taking in the morning, they generally commence about that time. During the day, unless there is a breeze of wind, little sport is to be had in the pools; but if there is a good ripple on them, very good sport may be had in the shallow water towards their lower end, as also in stretches of thin still water, which, at other times, it would be useless fishing. The whole of a pool may be fished when there is a breeze of wind upon it, but there is no part like the lower end, where there are always plenty of trout lying. When there is no wind, the only part of a pool worth fishing is the strong rush at the head. The streams, however, are what the angler should rely upon, and an experienced worm-fisher can tell almost with certainty where he will catch a trout. At this season, feeding trout are to be found in places which a novice would pass over as not worth fishing. The strong deep runs are by no means to be neglected, but the best trout are to be got in shallow water, at the edges of strong runs, where they lie, basking in the sun, and on anything disturbing them run into the current for shelter. They are also to be found in eddies behind stones, *below banks and tufts of grass;* in short, wherever they can lie unseen and watch for their prey as it comes down stream. Sometimes, also, particularly if the day is sunny, they will be found in thin quiet streams, and every run of water detached from the main current should be fished with great care. The best of all casts, however, are those where the river runs beneath the bank. When the waters continue small and clear for any length of time, the large trout become alarmed and seek for shelter, and it is in such places they are to be found.

In a stretch of thin, quiet, exposed water, you may depend upon every projecting piece of bank and every large stone sheltering a trout; and if there is a breeze you have every chance of securing some of them. The worm should be thrown about two yards above the place, and allowed to come down past it, if there is sufficient stream to carry it; if not, it should be drawn gently down. A stoppage of the line opposite the place will indicate the expected event. In large rivers we have fished with great success those places where the water is rapid but not very rough, between a pool and a very strong stream. Streams in the immediate neighbourhood of large pools will generally be found the best, as the trout come from the pools into the streams to feed.

At some periods of the day trout will not take so readily as at others, and there are times when they seem to leave off altogether, and will take nothing. The angler will generally find that, whatever he is fishing with, trout take most freely during what is usually called the time of the take, which generally happens in the early part of the day, and may be known by seeing the trout rising in numbers. It is evidently then that they are feeding, and they will take almost anything, but they leave off very suddenly, and we have been catching at the rate of three dozen trout an hour with the worm, when all at once, in the very best part of the water, they ceased taking our bait, and also rising at the natural insect, and for the next half hour we hardly stirred a fin. After a time of almost total stoppage, they will resume again, but not so freely as before.

A showery day with occasional sunshine, or an altogether sunny one without a cloud, is most favourable, but an entirely wet day is also very good. Very good sport may be had in calm thundery weather even with that bugbear "white clouds" in the sky, as also in blowy wet weather; but good sport is rarely to be met with on a dark windy day without rain, and the worst of all is a bright sky with a few clouds, and strong west wind. In such a day, early morning is the best time. A clear cloudless sky generally indicates a degree of frost in the atmosphere; and when this is the case, the trout do not take readily in the morning, until the heat of the sun begins to be felt. During the months of June and July we have frequently found that we could depend more upon sport when the wind was east than when it was west.

As July draws to a close, trout do not take the worm so well—they begin to be capricious, and will sometimes take only for an hour or two in the forenoon; so that worm-fishing in our earlier streams may be said to be at an end; and if the angler continues it through August, he must have recourse to the more backward districts; and sometimes even to hill-burns. We have known excellent worm-fishers unable to capture a dozen trout in the end of August, where a month earlier they could with ease have filled a basket. And worm-fishing may be limited to six weeks or two months in summer—the time varying according to the season, for which the best guide we can give the angler is, that it generally commences about a week after the May-flies are done, and in streams where these flies do not exist about the beginning of June.

All we have yet said on this head has applied *exclusively* to fishing when the waters are small and clear, and we shall now proceed to what remains of the subject—namely, angling with the worm in flooded waters and hill-burns.

To commence, then, with flooded waters. If the water is very heavy, one or two No. 3 split shot will be found an advantage. In such circumstances we generally use two common bait hooks, and tie the one about two feet above the other—

ANGLING IN FLOODED WATERS.

placing the shot between them about eight inches above the first hook. When the waters are very thick, worms will generally be found most enticing if newly taken from the earth, as in such circumstances trout are guided to them more by scent than sight, and a newly-dug worm has a much stronger smell than a long kept one.

The parts of the stream where sport may be expected in flooded waters are quite different from those which have been indicated as being suitable when the waters are reduced. Whenever a river begins to flood, trout seek the shallow sides of pools, and the thin and comparatively quiet water at the tails of streams, and in these places they will take the worm readily, until the river gets very large and thick, when they do not take readily, and lie in the eddies a few feet from the edge, keeping as much as possible out of reach of the current. The time when the particles of mud in the water begin to settle, and the water is of a brown colour, is the best of any. The trout now begin to move a little farther out, but are still in the moderately quiet water, and here the angler must still look for them.

There is no occasion for fishing up in a flooded water; the thickness of the water prevents the trout from seeing the angler; and the best plan is to commence at the top of a pool or stream, keeping on the shallow side, and throwing in your bait, follow it down to the foot, when you may repeat the process, or seek for some other place. If you are fishing the edge of a pool, where you know there are plenty of trout, you should keep at it for some time, particularly if the river is a large one. In a full flood there are not many places suitable for fishing, and the angler will frequently find that, if he starts at a good place, he will gain nothing by shifting his quarters.

When the river becomes of a dark porter colour, it is better to put off the sinkers, and fish up stream, and several excellent worm-fishers never use sinkers at all. But when the rivers are very thick, we think the advantages of sinkers considerably exceed the disadvantages, as without them the trout, which are guided to the bait by smell, would seldom see it at all, or if they did, it might be swept away before they had time to seize it.

In flooded waters trout may be captured with worm during the whole angling season, but more readily in June and July than in any of the other months. And if in either of these months there is a long tract of dry weather, and a small flood follows it, an immense quantity of trout may be caught, as after their long fast they will take with the greatest avidity. When the rivers continue small for a long time, the large trout get alarmed, and hide themselves below stones and banks, from which they do not stir, at least in the day-time. A flood, however, sets them all astir again, and more large trout may then be captured than in any other condition of the water, which is a considerable inducement, notwithstanding the coarseness of the practice, to try it occasionally. When several floods occur in succession about the month of July, trout become gorged with worms, and do not take at all readily, either during the time of the flood or even when the waters are once more in bait-fishing order—small and clear; apparently they get enough of worms to satisfy them for the season. In flooded waters, the morning will generally be found the best time, unless in the early part of the season, when the heat of the day is always favourable.

Fishing with the worm in hill-burns, like fishing in flooded waters, is not a very attractive sport, and requires but little of the skill necessary for successful worm-fishing in rivers and waters when they are small and clear. If the banks of the burn are open—that is to say, if it runs over a stony channel—the best way is to use a short rod and fish up in the usual manner. But if, as is frequently the case, the banks almost meet over the burn, the only plan is to drop the worm in and follow it down. There is no danger of the trout seeing you, as in such circumstances they are always under the banks. Every place where there is water to cover a trout should be fished, and we have seen trout nearly half a-pound weight caught in burns little larger than a sheep-drain, but they are invariably ugly, black, and ill-conditioned, and not worth the trouble of carrying home. Burns may be fished most successfully after rain; and as they are generally in late districts, August will be found the best month, but some sport may be had the whole season through, as the trout are invariably hungry.

CHAPTER VIII.

MAY-FLY FISHING.

THERE are two flies to which the term May-fly is applied. The first, which is known by anglers generally as the May-fly, is the green drake, a large yellowish fly, which makes its appearance on some streams in great numbers, from the middle to the end of June. Trout are very fond of them, seizing greedily every unlucky individual that ventures on the water; and a couple of them put on a small hook, and allowed to play on the surface, will be found very effective, particularly in woody places. It is subject, however, to the great objection of being almost as difficult to catch as the trout themselves; so that as far as angling, at least in Scotland, is concerned, it hardly deserves attention.

The second fly, which is known on Tweedside and in the Border districts as the May-fly, is the phryganea or stone-fly of naturalists; and when we speak of May-fly in the subsequent parts of this chapter or volume, it is this fly to which we allude. Away from Tweedside, its virtues as a lure for trout are little known, and we believe there are numbers of anglers who have never heard of it, and a still greater number who would not know it if they saw it. Unfortunately for the angler, the period of its duration in its matured state is short, but while it lasts it is a most deadly bait for trout; and, under circumstances favourable to its use, a greater weight can be taken by it than by fly, worm, or minnow. The trout captured by it are also larger than those caught by any other means, and in point of condition they are the very finest the river contains; indeed, with this bait, the angler will never get an ill-conditioned fish.

Mr. Wilson in the *Encyclopædia Britannica*, and again in the *Rod and Gun*, states that the stone-fly comes out of the caddis or case-worm; an aquatic larva, which is to be found plentifully in the bottom of most rivers, enclosed in a curious shell made of sticks and gravel cemented together. But we believe this distinguished naturalist to be in error; the caddis worms, or cod-bait, as they are usually denominated, are to be found in abundance up to the beginning of August, long after the last May-fly has disappeared, and are the larvæ of flies which assume the winged state during that month. In another part of his volume, Mr. Wilson alludes to the creeper or water-cricket as a bait deserving the attention of the angler; this is the stone or

CREEPER-FISHING.

May-fly in its embryo state, and a very deadly bait it is.

Creepers are to be found in the rivers all winter, but it is not till April that they merit the attention of the angler. They then vary in length from three-quarters to an inch and a quarter, are covered with a thin brown shell mottled yellow and black, have numerous legs, and are upon the whole the most venomous-looking insects that the angler in pursuit of his vocation encounters. They are to be found plentifully about the shallow parts of the water under stones, but run so quickly, that it requires some dexterity to catch them, as, unless the water is quite still, it is difficult to see them distinctly. About the middle of May, the time varying according to the season, the creeper leaves the water, where it has hitherto had its dwelling, and crawls on the dry stones, where it casts its shell, and assumes the winged state. The cast-off shells may be seen on the dry channel in great numbers; and by turning over the stones in such places, the flies may be had in abundance. The full-grown flies are generally about an inch long, and have large wings, which lie flat on the back, but seem of little use, as they invariably trust to their legs for safety. They are of a brownish colour, with a yellow tinge on the belly, and the wings are veined and almost transparent.

Whether the angler intends using the creeper or the fly, he should collect a sufficient number the night before he expects to use them. They are better newly gathered; but when the angler is fishing, unless he has an attendant, the gathering of them consumes much valuable time. The most convenient method of taking them to the water-side is in a tin case, shaped something like a powder-flask. It should be commodious, six or seven inches long by four or five wide, and an inch and a half thick. The end at which the flies are to be put in and taken out should be narrow, with an opening just sufficient to allow one or two flies to come out at a time, otherwise the angler will have great difficulty in keeping them in. The lid should be fastened with a hinge, and the whole canister perforated with holes to admit the air. The creepers can be best preserved in a little of the river water, and seem amphibious, as they will live a whole day in a canister in the angler's pocket. It is different with the flies; care must be taken to keep them dry, as water kills them.

Creepers, then, first merit the attention of the angler, and may be used with success as soon as trout come into condition. The rod and tackle used for worm-fishing will answer very well for this also, with the exception of the hook; and with regard to it, some anglers bait both the creeper and the fly on an ordinary-sized bait hook. We, however, think two hooks are best, and for creeper-fishing, use two No. 7 or 8 hooks tied with yellow silk to the same piece of gut, so close, that the barb

METHOD OF USING THE CREEPER.

of the one may be about half-an-inch distant from the barb of the other. Selecting a middle-sized creeper—the best are not the largest, but the yellowest—take the lower hook and put it through the creeper crossways a little above the tail, then take the upper hook, and put it through about the shoulder, according as the size of the creeper suits the tackle. Two hooks possess this advantage over one, that the second hook prevents the creeper from slipping down on the shank of the hook, which, when one hook is used, it always does. In large rivers such as Tweed, or rivers inhabited by large trout, it may be advisable to use two creepers, in which case they should be baited in the same manner, and upon the same tackle as will subsequently be recommended for the May-fly. The creeper should be used in the same manner as a worm—fishing up stream without a sinker, and in the same kind of water, which, as we have fully described in worm-fishing, it is unnecessary to repeat here. The only difference is, that whereas the angler will frequently catch trout with the worm in moderately still water, he will scarcely ever catch one with the creeper, and should therefore confine his operations entirely to strong water. The state of water and weather most suitable is exactly the same as that looked upon with most favour by the worm-fisher—a small clear water and a sunny day, with a breeze. The best time of day entirely depends upon the weather; if the weather is mild, trout will take readily early in the morning, but in cold weather they do not commence till 8 or 9 A.M., and leave off in about five or six hours.

The creeper in general will not be found effective until trout are thoroughly in condition, as, until they are so, they have not strength to lie in the streams, where alone this bait is of any use. The longer they remain on the water, the more readily trout take them. They are a much more deadly bait in the middle of May than in the middle of April, and when they are changing into flies, we have found it quite immaterial whether we used the creeper or the fly.

The May-fly is even a more deadly bait than the creeper; but unfortunately the period of its duration is shorter. If the flies can be got of sufficient size, they may be baited in the same manner as the creeper, if intended to be used among small trout when the streams are clear; but in any other circumstances two should be used; and they should be baited in the following manner, substituting for the lower hook of the creeper tackle a larger hook, say a No. 5 or 6 :—Take a good-sized fly, and, entering the large hook about the middle, run it along the body, and bring it out at the tail; then run the fly up the shank of the large hook, and insert the small hook through its shoulders, which will keep it in position; next

METHOD OF USING THE MAY-FLY.

take another fly, and, entering the large hook a little above the middle, bring it out a little below. If two flies do not cover the hooks properly, the angler should put on three. They are very tender, and must be used with great delicacy, as the least jerk in casting will break them; and if the angler strikes, he will require to bait anew, as the mere drawing through the water mutilates them.

The flies float upon the surface of the water, so that they cannot be used exactly like a bait, but are used in a similar manner. Casting them up from him, the angler should allow them to come down a short distance, and then cast again farther up. If the flies are coming down with their wings out of the water, the trout make a fair rise at them, but, what is rather singular, and quite unaccountable, rarely take a proper hold. It is better to have the flies thoroughly soaked and under the surface, when the trout take them in a much more deadly manner; and the first indication the angler sometimes receives is a stoppage of the line, when he should slacken for a moment or two; then strike down stream, and be very careful in landing, as the fish thus taken are always large and strong.

If the water is clear, the angler should fish in the same places as with the creeper, with this difference, that he will meet with success in the streamy portions of pools, casting up stream to within half-a-foot of the deep edge. The best casts, however, in any condition of water, are where the stream runs below the bank. There trout may be depended upon, if the angler casts to within a foot of the edge; and as the current is not so strong at the edge as a foot further out, the angler must endeavour to keep his line out of the main current, or his flies will come down too fast. Unlike the creeper, the May-fly is most killing when the waters are large and dark-coloured, and must then be used close to the edges; the angler will seldom get a trout in the centre of the current. The deep and strong sides of pools and streams, within a foot of the edge, are the best places; but every spot where a tuft of grass or projecting bush or bank affords shelter to a trout should be fished with great care. A rapid sweep of water past some dry channel can always be relied upon, as the channel produces flies in abundance, and some trout are sure to be on the outlook for them. Greater nicety in casting is requisite in using this bait than any others, as, if the angler casts half-a-foot too far out, when the waters are flooded, his labour will be in vain. When the waters are clear, trout will occasionally take in the centre of the stream; but the edges are always mostly to be depended upon, as the trout wishing to feed upon the May-flies come to the edges to look for them.

Trout generally take May-fly best early in the

morning; but if much dew has fallen during the night, they will not take freely until the sun has dried it up. There are usually two distinct takes with this bait; one in the morning, from about three to six, when they stop for a short time, but resume again in an hour or two, and continue taking for four or five hours. They take again in the evening, but not so readily. A bright sunny day, with a breeze or a thoroughly wet one, we consider most favourable.

Trout take the May-fly most readily when it has been about a week on the water; and should a small flood occur, they will take voraciously. If a heavy flood occurs when the flies are all out, it will carry them away, and finish May-fly fishing for the season. The beginning of June is generally the time when this fishing is at its prime; about the middle of the month, or even sooner, the flies get scarce, and the angler must, with great regret, have recourse to something else. For the time it lasts it is splendid sport. The trout are of large size, and being in prime condition, run most vigorously, and test to the utmost both the angler's skill and tackle. There are some rivers where the flies are not to be had; and unless there are plenty of stones, they are never found in great numbers; but where they are, trout take them in any size of water, from Tweed to the smallest hill-burn.

Cod-bait, maggots, and the larvæ of some other

insects, are very much esteemed by some anglers as baits for trout; but, for our own part, we have always found a clear red worm more effective. It is also more easily got, and certainly more agreeable to handle.

CHAPTER IX.

MINNOW AND PARR-TAIL FISHING.

THIS is a very inviting branch of the art. No method of trout-fishing exercises a more lively influence over the angler's hopes and fears, or requires the exercise of so much presence of mind, as trouting with the minnow or parr-tail; a large trout makes a glorious rush at a minnow, and it requires both skill and coolness in order to secure it. Like other methods of angling, minnow-fishing in discoloured water is comparatively easy, and in such circumstances it is better understood by those who practise it than any other branch of the art; but when the streams are clear, to fish successfully with the minnow, particularly in small waters, requires great dexterity, and is one of the most difficult operations of angling.

One great inducement to use the minnow is the large size of the trout captured. The largest trout taken by the rod are usually caught with it, but the average is not equal in size and still less in condition to these captured with the May-fly. Trout accustomed to prey upon their neighbours usually attain great size, and may be more readily taken by the minnow than by any other means; but these overgrown specimens are generally not inviting.

The value of the minnow, however, as a lure for trout is to some extent lessened by the difficulty of procuring them. In places and circumstances most favourable to their use, it is sometimes impossible to get them, and we have frequently found the capture of minnows much more difficult than the capture of the trout when we had got them; their capture, therefore, becomes an object of primary consideration.

Minnows are not easily caught till April, as it is not till the streams are in some measure reduced that they venture out from under the banks and other places where they have sheltered themselves from the torrents of winter. In most of the streams in the south of Scotland they are to be found in abundance from April to November. They frequent the thin edges of pools, and every place where a turn of the river leaves a corner, or as it is called "back water," where they can swim unmolested; and in a sunny day such places may be seen almost black with them.

A great many different contrivances are employed to capture them. The small pout or landing-net may be used very effectively during the time of a flood, and it should be worked with the current about the edges of places which the minnows are known to frequent, and in back water. It may also be employed when a shoal of minnows is found in some detached piece of water; in which case the mud should be stirred up before commencing, when they may be captured with great ease.

When a shoal of minnows is in a corner, they may be captured without much difficulty. The small hoop-net will secure a good many, but a much more efficient plan is to have a net tied between two sticks, about two feet separate, with the lower end of the net leaded. This is wrought quickly up into the corner, and as it lies close to the bottom, very few minnows escape. By this means as many minnows may be taken at a single haul as will last a week. This is the only kind of net we carry with us when angling, as it goes into little bulk, and a couple of sticks with which to use it can be picked up at the water-side.

The great difficulty, however, lies in catching minnows when they are in the open stream. For this purpose we use an oblong net, about two yards wide and as many long. This should be attached to two sticks, with the lower side of the net leaded, and a few corks put on the upper side, so as to get as much opening as possible. The angler should then place it at the side of some stream where the minnows are, and chase them into it. That is the most reliable of all the methods of capturing minnows. A net of the size just mentioned, with the mesh sufficiently small, would cost several pounds; but a piece of light canvas, which will do equally well, and of which we make all our nets, may be got from any seedsman for a mere trifle.

A very ingenious method of capturing minnows is practised by anglers in Aberdeenshire, but whether or not our northern friends can claim the merit of the invention we cannot say. It consists of a clear glass bottle of the structure indicated in the accompanying illustration.

It is used in this way :—A piece of open canvas, or what is preferable, small-meshed net, is tied over the mouth, and a few crumbs of bread put into the interior. The bottle is then placed in some stream which the minnows frequent, with the mouth to the stream. The water rushing in agitates the crumbs and so attracts the minnows, which collect about the bottom of the bottle, and being naturally of an inquiring turn of mind, gradually find their way up to the opening at *a*, where they enter, and, fascinated by the all-powerful attractions of the bottle, remain, and in a few minutes there will be two or three dozen in the interior. The objections to the use of the bottle are of course that it is very inconvenient to carry, and very liable to be broken; but anglers cannot have everything just to their

METHODS OF CAPTURING MINNOWS. 177

mind, and anything is better than running short of minnows; and when any difficulty occurs in this respect we would counsel an immediate application to the bottle. We have started to fish with minnow in the early morning without a minnow in our box. Arrived at the water-side we set our bottle, and then put up our rod; by the time this was done the bottle had secured a dozen, which we commenced fishing with, and then set the bottle again. Now this is very convenient, and wastes less time than any other method of catching minnows, and for the minnow-fisher the bottle is a great invention.

When minnows are intended to be used immediately, they may be captured with a small hook. The best way of doing this is to take a hook, and attach to its shank three or four small pieces of gut, with a pair of small hooks, say No. 11, attached to each, which should hang from an inch to an inch and a half below the single hook. This latter is then baited with a small piece of red worm; and when the minnows are clustered about it, it is pulled out with a jerk, and the angler will generally get two or three minnows hooked by the outside of the body. The object of this is to get small minnows, as the bait is usually seized by the large ones, to the exclusion of those which the angler wishes to capture.

Those anglers who have the command of a piece of water can always keep a supply of live minnows by enclosing them in a wire box, which should be sunk to the bottom of the water by a weight, and raised when the minnows are wanted. But as numbers of anglers do not reside at the water-side, and when engaged in a day's trouting cannot afford to spend half of it in catching minnows, they should always be provided with a plentiful supply of salted ones, which will be found much more deadly than the best imitations that ever were made. As minnows shrivel up considerably when salted, a size larger should be selected for this purpose than those intended to be used fresh. If meant to be used within four or five days they should be put in the strongest pickle, and they will be almost as good as fresh; but if not used in a few days, they become soft and quite useless. For keeping they should be placed in a jar, with layers of salt between them, and the brine poured off as it accumulates.

The great objections to salted minnows are, that they dry into mere skins, so that it is exceedingly difficult to get them to spin properly; and that they are very tender, requiring great care in using, and even with the greatest care they will not last long; and the angler, if possible, should always be provided with a plentiful supply of live ones, as they are undoubtedly the best. For containing them when angling there is nothing better than an oblong tin box (the invention of a very ingenious angler, the late Mr. Darling of Edinburgh), which

SIZE OF MINNOW.

can be strapped round the waist, and is so constructed that the shaking of the box does not spill the water. Five or six dozen minnows may be kept alive in one of them for a whole day by changing the water occasionally. Those that die should be allowed to remain in the water, as they will keep fresher and firmer there than elsewhere.

A minnow measuring about an inch and three-quarters, total length, tail inclusive, is the size we prefer for trouting at all seasons; and small minnows are now most commonly used by all able minnow-fishers. A large trout will take a small minnow as readily as a large one, a middle-sized trout more so, and a small trout, which could not take a large minnow, will take a small one readily. In the spring of the year, before trout come into condition, or in autumn, when they are again out of it, a large minnow may answer; or even in summer, when the waters are flooded, a middle-sized minnow may prove inviting; but in streams inhabited by well-fed trout, when they are low and clear, minnows cannot be used too small if they will turn the swivels. A large minnow spins in a clumsy, unsightly manner, very different from the neat turning of a small one. Trout, also, can get hold of a small minnow much more easily than of a large one, and so the angler has a much better chance of hooking them. The whitest and most slivery minnows should always be selected; those that are of a greenish colour underneath being almost worthless.

For trouting with the minnow the rod should be double-handed, not less than fifteen or sixteen feet; and in order to throw the minnow with the additions of swivels and shot properly, it must be stiff. The reel, line, and casting-line in common use will answer very well for this also. It is the common practice to dress minnow-tackle on gut strong enough to draw out a salmon by main force, as if the trout, which requires the finest gut to deceive it when angling with the fly, would seize a minnow at the end of a rope. The argument used in favour of this practice is, that it lasts the longer, as no doubt it does; but what is the use of tackle lasting that will not catch? and the strong white glittering gut upon which minnow-tackles are usually tied is quite sufficient, when the waters are clear, to frighten away three trout out of four. That the gut used for minnow-tackles must be a little stronger than that used for flies is quite true, but a very little difference will do; if it is so strong that the spinning of the minnow does not twist it, it is all that is necessary.

With regard to the number of hooks of which the minnow-tackle should consist, great diversity of opinion exists. Some use only two, while others use four, five, six, and even seven. We have tried all varieties, and think that two hooks with a drag behind will kill more than any other combination ; and two, or at most three, hooks are now most commonly used by those whose opinion is worth having. There are occasions when, from the trout biting shy, the angler may raise ten trout, and not secure one. On such occasions we have found a drag, consisting of two No. 10 hooks tied back to back, and left to play loose about three inches behind the minnow, very effective. Some anglers put a drag-hook about half-an-inch behind the tail, in expectation of those trout that bite short taking hold of this hook with their mouth, but this rarely happens. The tail of the minnow in spinning describes a considerable circumference, and the drag, being farther out, a still greater one ; so that, if the trout misses the minnow, there is little chance of its catching the drag. The drag which we advise should be dressed on a separate piece of gut, sufficiently long to keep it at least three inches behind the minnow, and attached to the upper hook of the minnow-tackle by a loop, so that it may be taken off or put on at pleasure. The object of having it so far behind the minnow is to catch, by the outside of the body, those trout which bite shy, or miss the minnow.

In order to test whether the two hooks by themselves, or with the addition of the drag, kill most, we fished for several days, time about with each—having the drag on one half-hour and off the next. We have, unfortunately, lost our notes on the subject, but the result was decidedly in favour of a drag. Sometimes more than half of what we caught were taken by it; at others not more than a third. When the drag was on, we did not catch so many trout on the minnow-tackle itself, as when the drag was off, which we account for in two ways. Firstly, the drag is likely to alarm a few trout which would otherwise take the minnow; and secondly and mainly, the drag captured at the first rise numbers of trout which would have repeated their attack and been caught by the minnow-tackle proper. On no occasion did we catch more without the drag than with it, but we think it quite possible, that in very clear water, and among very wary trout, the drag might alarm them; and that if it is not catching a fair proportion—say at least one in four—it may safely be dispensed with.

The following illustration shows the minnow-

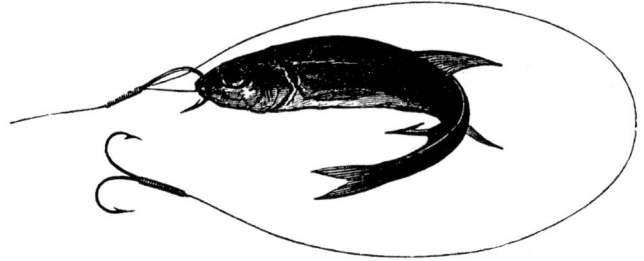

tackle, and also a view of the minnow when baited.

In baiting, take the large hook, and, entering it

METHOD OF BAITING THE MINNOW.

at the mouth of the minnow, run it right through the body, and bring it out about a quarter of an inch from the tail, leaving the minnow as nearly as possible in the curve represented in the foregoing figure. The object of having the minnow in a curve form is, that it may turn round when it is drawn against the stream, and this can be better accomplished by a small curvature than a large one. If the body of the minnow is almost doubled up, the spinning is horrible to behold, and much more likely to alarm than attract a trout; the smallest curvature will do, and the hook should protrude freely. The upper hook is then stuck through the lips, which completes the process, and the angler should, before commencing, draw it through the water, to see that it spins properly.

Some anglers use a much larger hook for the lips than we have indicated; acting upon the prevalent opinion that trout invariably seize and swallow their prey head-foremost, and that there should therefore be a large hook there. So far as our experience goes, this opinion is incorrect. We have frequently caught trout with numbers of minnows and other small fish in their inside, nine out of ten of which were swallowed tail-foremost; and this is only natural, as it is hardly to be supposed that a minnow will look a trout in the face till the latter swallows him; and it is equally improbable that the trout will let the minnow out of his mouth when once in, merely for the gratification of bolting him head-foremost. From observations taken when the water was clear, we think that five trout out of six seize the minnow from behind. We have watched them come out from below the opposite bank, and follow the minnow across, always keeping below it, apparently afraid that they might be seen by their prey, and frequently making no attempt to seize it till it was just at the edge. Some anglers say that the upper hook is the most deadly, but we have never found this to be the case, generally capturing four trout on the lower hook for one on the upper : and even when caught with the upper wire, the appearance frequently shows that they have had the whole minnow in their mouth, and that the upper hook had first come in contact with their mouth in striking, but that the lower hook and the minnow had been expelled subsequently to their being hooked. A large hook through the lips is very easily seen, and also interferes with the spinning of the minnow.

Swivels are a necessary addition to the minnow-tackle in order to prevent the spinning of the minnow from twisting the line. One should be placed about two feet above the hook, and a second about a yard farther up. Split shot, Nos. 2 and 3, are also necessary to the minnow-fisher, and should be placed above the first swivel. Some place them below, but in this position they interfere very much with the spinning of the minnow, as it has to turn round two or three split shot, which, unless a large minnow, it cannot do properly.

Minnow-fishing in flooded waters is so different from minnow-fishing when the waters are clear, that we shall treat of them separately, and shall commence with the flooded waters. The mode of fishing usually adopted is to throw the minnow across the stream, and work it gradually round, now pulling it up the water for a foot or so, and then letting it fall back again, and so on, till it comes round to the side on which the angler is standing. It should be subjected to every variety of motion, one cast drawn steadily against the stream, and the next with short jerks across it; and even allowing it to go with the current will sometimes prove inviting. Great care should be taken not to lift the minnow out of the water till it is quite close to the edge, as trout will frequently follow the minnow, and make no attempt to seize it until it is just at the edge, when, apparently afraid that their prey is about to escape, they make a rush at it. When a trout has taken the minnow the line should be slackened for a moment or two, to allow it to get the minnow fairly in its mouth, and then the angler should strike firmly. Fly-fishers are exceedingly apt to strike the moment they feel or see anything, which is much too soon. For this reason also a moderately long line is advantageous, as with it the angler cannot strike so soon, and as he is fishing down stream it has also the advantage of keeping him out of sight.

The time of a flood when trout take the minnow most readily is when the water is just beginning to rise, and is of a whitish colour. Then it is that the large trout begin to bestir themselves, and leave the banks and stones where they have been hiding, when the waters were clear, to roam about the sides of pools and the tails of streams; and here it is that the angler should look for them. When the river is in full flood little can be done, but on its beginning to subside, when the particles of mud are settling, but the water is not yet of the dark porter colour, trout will again take the minnow readily, and in the same places—the ebb sides of pools, and tails of streams. When the waters are in this state, large trout may sometimes be seen rising at the fly close to the edge, on the deep side of the water; in such circumstances they will take a minnow readily. Sufficient shot should be used when the streams are swollen to keep the minnows well under water, as by doing so it is more likely to be seen, and the light being less the character of the lure is not so easily detected.

In flooded waters trout take the minnow during the whole of the angling season, but more readily in May, June, and July than in any other months. In May the forenoon is the best time, but in June and July, if the weather is mild, the morning from three to eight is usually the best time; but if the weather is stormy, trout will take most readily during the day. A flooded water during June or

July is a sure index of sport, and should be attended to.

Trouting with the minnow when the waters are clear is a much more difficult and elegant practice than that just described. If the water is sufficiently deep to admit of it, the minnow should be kept well sunk, as it spins better; and as the angler cannot see the trout take it, he is therefore less likely to strike too soon. In large streams, the necks of pools, rapid broken water of no great depth, detached currents, and the comparatively smooth but strong water at the foot of pools, are in general the best places. Unless the trout are taking very readily, we have never met with much sport in deep water of any kind.

In small streams, when they are clear, it is better to dispense with sinkers, as they make a great splash on alighting, and in shallow water are exceedingly apt to drag the minnow to the bottom. In small streams the main current and strong runs at pool heads are likely places, but the best casts of all are where the stream runs beneath the bank, even though the water is comparatively quiet. The angler should throw his minnow upon the opposite bank, and drawing it gently off, spin it past the place where he expects the trout is lying, and across to his own side of the water. He may frequently observe the trout come out from the opposite bank, and again and again make a dart at the minnow, and turn back; if he gives his minnow a jerk, which it requires considerable practice to refrain from doing, ten chances to one but he alarms the trout; he should continue playing his minnow in the same manner, and never lift it till it is close to the edge. He must also avoid moving, as the trout, having started from some place where it could not see him, follows the minnow till it comes within sight of him; so long, however, as he remains stationary there is nothing to alarm it, but if he makes any movement it will bolt off immediately.

Even in shallow still water, if there is any projecting piece of bank which can afford shelter to a trout, the angler may capture it if there is the least ripple on the water, but such casts require to be fished very carefully and without a sinker. In rivers much fished with the minnow we frequently get most trout in these out-of-the-way places, as most anglers pass them over as unworthy of notice.

In small streams, when they are clear and low, we have fished up stream with minnow with great success. All still and even moderately-quiet waters can be fished just as easily up stream as down, and by adopting this method, using fine tackle without a drag and small minnows, we have captured trout in mill-caulds and other places with no stream in them, when the sun was shining brightly and not a ripple on the surface. Even in streams, if the angler throws his minnow partly across and partly up, and just pulls it towards him, trout will take it readily. The best sport we ever had was by fishing up stream with the minnow and worm alternately.

The minnow may also be baited and used in the same manner as a worm—a small minnow is best for this method; but we have never met with much success by using it in this way, and the sport is not nearly so attractive as ordinary minnow fishing.

Trout may be captured with minnow, when the waters are clear, during the whole season, but the summer quarter is the best. In the month of May, trout generally take most readily in the afternoon, from two or three to six, or even later; but in June and July, the early morning, and the evening from a little before sunset till midnight, and sometimes on till daylight, are the best times. Should, however, the weather be very coarse, it is useless fishing either in the morning or at night, and the trout will take most readily during the early part of the day.

At all seasons, and at all hours, and in all conditions of water—unless, perhaps, in a full flood, when an occasional blink of sunshine is beneficial—we prefer dark weather for trouting with the minnow; and in June and July the weather can hardly be too coarse.

In warm summer nights the minnow is a very deadly bait, and should be fished with in quiet still water, and about the shallow water at the foot and edges of pools, as trout cruise about among such places all night.

The parr-tail may almost be considered as a substitute for the minnow, and it is a very deadly lure for large trout in large rivers, particularly when they are flooded, but in small streams we have never found it of much use. It is unnecessary to instruct the reader in the method of capturing parr; in Tweed, or any other stream where they are numerous, he will generally get far more than he wishes. They frequent the thin water, and take most readily in a sunny day.

The tackle used for parr-tail should be of the same kind as that used for minnow, but with larger hooks, say a No. 1 for the lower hook, and a No. 5 for the upper, with a drag attached as in a minnow-tackle.

The following illustration shows the most approved method of cutting and baiting the parr.

Divide the parr across from A to B, and cut off all the fins till it resembles the second figure, then take the large hook, and entering it at the tail run it along the back and out at the other end, curving the bait to make it spin.

Some anglers bait the parr-tail in the reverse manner from what we have indicated, thinking it is more natural looking, but when so put on it rarely spins well, and never lasts long; whereas, baited with the small end to the line, it will spin

METHOD OF BAITING THE PARR-TAIL. 191

for hours. A parr-tail, bait it any way you please, resembles nothing in life; and the only object to be aimed at is, as in minnow-fishing, by rapid

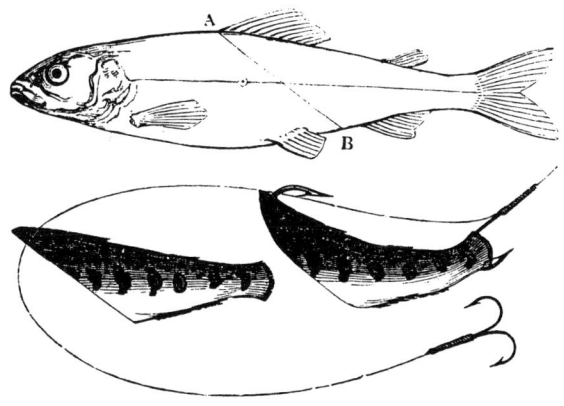

spinning to conceal the tackle and create an appearance of life.

Thus baited, it should be used in the same manner as a minnow, and among casts of the same description. The two conditions of water most favourable for the use of minnow are also those most favourable for the use of parr-tail, either when the waters are swollen, or when they are small and clear. Sometimes trout will take minnow more readily than parr-tail, and sometimes, we are informed, though we have never experienced it, they will take parr-tail more readily than minnow; but for our own part we never use parr-tail when we can get minnows.

CHAPTER X.

LOCH FISHING.

ANGLING in lochs is not held in such estimation as angling in running water. There is a tiresome monotony in fishing continually in still water, where the angler must ply his lure unremittingly in the same manner. There is no whirling eddy, no rippling stream, no projecting bush or bank, where, if the angler casts neatly, he is almost sure to be rewarded for his skill; the nicety in casting, so essential in order to fish a river successfully, being here almost entirely dispensed with. Nor is there much room for bringing into play knowledge of the habits of the trout, local knowledge almost entirely superseding it; for the angler, guided by a boatman who is familiar with every bay or bank where sport may be expected, has merely to throw his line, and the only skill requisite is in striking and landing a trout. Fishing from the bank, if the angler is without attendant, requires more knowledge of the habits of the trout than fishing from a boat, as the angler has to find out for himself the places in which to fish; but with all his skill, he can never tell with any certainty which is a good bay and which a bad one, nor can he tell, as in a river, at what cast to expect a trout.

The trout also, from a variety of causes, are not so wary or difficult of capture as the wily inhabitants of most streams. Highland lochs are generally of a dark colour, which helps to disguise the angler's tackle; and as the trout are little fished for, and rarely disturbed, they are by no means shy.

All these things render loch-fishing a less difficult, and consequently less interesting, branch of angling than fishing in our southern streams. It is, indeed, the simplest fishing of any, and the one in which the tyro and the accomplished angler are most upon a par; and we do not wonder that most good anglers prefer capturing smaller but more wary trout in southern streams, to larger and better trout in some remote loch.

Still loch-fishing has its advantages. It is not nearly so fatiguing as river-fishing, and therefore better adapted for some. A sail on a loch possesses great attractions, and as many of our lochs are situated amidst the finest and grandest scenery in the country, the angler must indeed be destitute of taste if he can find no enjoyment in it. In an angling point of view, great inducements to fish in lochs are the large size and fine condition of the trout. In this last respect they certainly surpass those that are found in rivers, being in some lochs quite equal, if not superior, to the salmon itself, and cutting much redder in the flesh.

Most of those acquainted with the subject are of opinion that loch-trout are of the same species as those which are found in rivers, and that their distinctive characteristics are entirely the result of feeding. In some lochs, in addition to the common trout, the *Salmo ferox* is found—a large coarse species, chiefly predatory in its habits, but affording excellent play when hooked. This fish is occasionally caught of great size, and numbers have been caught weighing from ten to twenty pounds. One was caught in 1866 by William Muir, Esq., of Innistrynich, which completely surpasses any that we have ever heard of. This patriarch of the species weighed $39\frac{1}{2}$ pounds, and measured 3 feet 9 inches in length, and 2 feet $2\frac{1}{4}$ inches in girth.

What is remarkably strange, it was taken by Mr. Muir *with fly*, when engaged in angling for salmon in the river Awe, where it leaves the loch of the same name, and landed after a run of upwards of two hours, during which Mr. Muir had to cross the river in a boat which fortunately was at hand. What age this fish was it is impossible to conjecture. It was, as its dimensions prove, a well-conditioned fish, and had the curvature of the upper jaw— which is usually considered to betoken age—very strongly developed. Conjecture and imagination would be alike at fault in reckoning what number of lines, of all descriptions, this monster must have seen in his time. The amount of learning in such matters which he must have accumulated during a residence in the loch of probably not less than fifty years, he put to a miserable use in the end— selling himself for a very small mess of pottage indeed, as it was a small salmon-fly with which Mr. Muir accomplished the feat. His taking, or rather attempting to take, the fly at all—as though hooked outside the jaw he rose at it—can be accounted for on no other supposition than that old age had weakened his intellect, and impaired his memory. Mr. Muir very properly got him stuffed, with the fatal hook still in his jaw.

The common trout in lochs may be captured by any of the methods usually employed in rivers, but the only one of these that can be called sport, and the one that undoubtedly deserves the first notice, is the artificial fly.

The notion usually entertained, that some particular fly is necessary for every different loch— that a fly will not take unless its body is made of some particular dubbing, its wing of some particular feather, and that the least deviation from rule in the colour even of the tail-tuft will injure its usefulness—we believe to be altogether erroneous. The prevailing opinion, that in order to be successful the artificial fly must be an imitation of some one of the natural flies on the water at the time, will also, when applied to loch-fishing, be found absurd. We should like to know what insects the gaudy-coloured loch-flies in common use are intended to represent, or what part of the body it is that is imitated by the tinsel so lavishly bestowed. Certainly, we ourselves never saw any insects like artificial loch-flies.

It is quite unnecessary to have a large collection of flies, and the following comprise all that are necessary for any loch in which trout are to be found :—Red, purple, orange, yellow, blue, brown, and green bodies, made either of Berlin wool or mohair, and with or without tinsel. Wings of feathers taken from the jay, woodcock, grouse, teal, or mallard (we prefer the three first mentioned), with black and red cock-hackles, or the small feathers alluded to when treating of river-flies, varied to suit the colour of the fly. A tail is an improvement to the appearance of a good-sized fly, and may be made of a few fibres of the feathers taken from the neck of the golden pheasant, or a tuft of Berlin wool of a different colour from the body of the fly. In loch as in river fishing, the angler must be cautioned against trusting too much in flies.

In dressing loch-flies, the hackle may either be carried down the full length of the body, or confined to the part immediately below the wings; the latter is perhaps preferable, as it makes a neater and more shapely fly. Commence operations at the bend of the hook—at the place where you intend the tail of the fly to be—by fastening on the tail-tuft, and the end of the thread of worsted or mohair, of which you are to form the body, also the end of the thread of tinsel. Then lay the gut along the shank of the hook, and tie them firmly together until within five or six turns of the end of the hook, where fasten on, and divide the wings in the usual way, seeing that they stand well apart; next fasten on the hackle, and turn it round frequently, as close under the wings as possible, giving the silk one or two turns round it to keep it secure, and cut off the remainder, as in dressing a small fly. Then take the thread of worsted, and wrap it firmly round up to where the hackle is, and give the thread a turn or two round it. All that now remains to be done is to wrap the tinsel firmly round the body up to the place where your silk thread is, which you should whip three or four times over all, and finish off as close to the wings as possible. Finishing under the wings makes a very neat fly, and if well done it is hardly possible to tell where it is finished. We do not know if this is the artistic mode of making a loch-fly, but it is the best way we know, and the following illustration shows what like they are when made.

Flies made of the materials already mentioned, and varied in size according to circumstances, are all that is necessary for loch-fishing in Scotland. To adapt the size to the circumstances is, however, a matter of no small difficulty. The same causes which regulate the angler in fixing the size of his

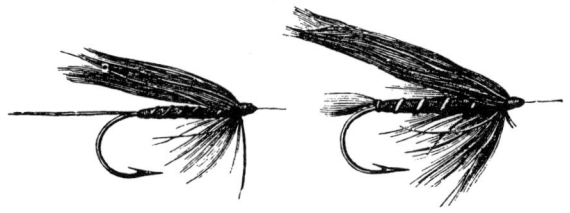

river-flies should be his guide here also. The great point at which to aim is to have a fly sufficiently large to insure its being seen, but not large enough to allow the trout to detect its artificiality. To accomplish this the angler who visits a number of lochs must be provided with all sizes of flies from No. 10 up to No. 3.

The colour of the water and the amount of wind are two of the principal causes which should regulate the angler in selecting the size of fly. If the water is dark-coloured, a size or two larger should be used than when it is clear. If there is a strong breeze of wind blowing, a size or two larger may be used than when there is little wind; and when there is no wind at all, we have found an approach to river sizes, say Nos. 9 and 10, most effective—always remembering to increase or diminish the size, according as the state of water and wind prevents the fly being easily seen or the reverse.

We once had a signal proof of what difference the wind will make, when fishing a loch from a boat, in company with a friend. We commenced with small-sized flies, and our friend with large ones. The breeze was very gentle when we began, and while it continued so, we captured six trout for our friend's one; but after we had been fishing for some time, it began to blow violently, when the tables were turned, leaving us behind. After waiting long enough to ascertain the point, we put on large flies, which put us both on an equal footing. The depth of water also, to a certain extent, regulates the size of fly. The trout in lochs usually lie near the bottom, and if the water is deep it will require a larger size of fly to attract their attention; but as it is usual for the angler to fish in about the same depth of water, there is no occasion for his troubling himself about this.

The colour of the water and the amount of wind should also, to some extent, regulate the colour of the fly. In dark-coloured lochs, red and the more gaudy colours will be found most enticing, while, in a clear water, brown and the more sober colours will be found best. Also, in a stormy day, a gaudy-coloured fly will answer best; but in a calm one, always choose the less glaring colours, and avoid tinsel.

The only other cause which should influence the angler in selecting the proper size and colour of flies is the wariness of the trout. Where trout are not at all shy, larger and more gaudy flies may be used than where they are much fished for, or shy from any cause, as a shy fish is very suspicious, and will detect the counterfeit in a smaller fly than another fish will. It is exceedingly difficult to regulate the size and colour of flies by theory, but in practice it is much simpler. Keeping the general principles in mind, the angler should commence with two or three different sizes and several different colours, and when he ascertains which is taking best, regulate accordingly. Just as in river-fishing it is advisable, if the trout evince a decided preference for one fly, to put on two or three of that description.

The gut upon which loch-flies are dressed, and by which the casts are made up, is in general far too thick. All the fine hanks are selected for river purposes, and the strong white glittering ones set aside for loch-fishing, as if gut could not be got sufficiently thick, and a loch-trout would seize a fly at the end of anything. It is quite true that stronger gut may be used with success in lochs than in rivers, yet the finer the gut the better the chance of success. In all kinds of angling, it is of the utmost importance to have the connecting link between the lure and the rod as little seen as possible. Their common use of thick gut is one of the reasons why anglers meet with no success when there is no wind, and with but little when there is only a gentle breeze. It is erring on the safe side to use fine gut, and we

ROD AND FLIES FOR LOCH-FISHING.

never yet got a hank of gut which we considered too fine for dressing loch-flies on. In some lochs we have caught more trout than anglers accustomed to fish them every day, simply because we used fine gut, and they used it very thick and white.

The rod for fly-fishing from a boat need not be longer than thirteen or fourteen feet, as that is long enough to keep the angler out of sight, and a very long rod is cumbrous to manage. In angling from the bank, a rod of two feet longer might be advisable, in order to reach the places where the trout lie. The reel should be large enough to contain fifty or sixty yards of line; for if you get a large fish, you must exhaust it by length of line, since you cannot follow it as on a river. But there is no occasion to have either the line or the triple-gut casting-line thicker than what is used for ordinary trouting purposes. A landing net is an almost indispensable article when fishing from a boat, and every angler should be provided with one.

The cast of flies should be made up in the usual manner, but as the flies are larger, the distance between them should be increased to about three feet. As to the number of flies to be used at a time, the angler may with safety use as many as he can manage properly; but we think that in fishing from a boat four will generally be found sufficient, as if there is a great number it is exceedingly difficult to prevent them from hankin below the boat when landing a trout. In fishing from the bank, the angler may use as many flies as he can throw out properly.

The great object in loch, as in river fishing, is to get over the ground quickly and thoroughly, if possible bringing your flies within range of every trout in the water you pass over. And as the first few yards of the flies' course is the most effective, you should cast frequently. When angling from the bank, the flies should be thrown straight out as far as possible, and then drawn gently towards the shore. If allowed to remain still the trout would at once discover the deception, to obviate which the flies must be always kept in motion; a slight jerking motion we have generally found most enticing. After the flies have traversed a few yards of water the angler should cast again a few yards further along, and so on, only casting once in the same place. When angling from a boat, the usual way is to place it with its side to the wind, and allow it to drift down; the boatman keeping it the requisite distance from the shore. If the breeze is strong, the boat will drift too fast to admit of fishing the water thoroughly, and a large stone attached to a rope should be put out at the windward side to act as a drag. Commencing at the bow of the boat the angler should first cast straight out, and then go gradually round, casting to leeward, and in a fresh piece of water

BEST PARTS OF A LOCH.

every time till he come to the stern, when he should begin again.

The parts of the loch in which to fish, as has been before stated, can only be ascertained with certainty by local experience. The amount of food is the principal cause which influences trout in their preference of one part of a loch to another, and this depends entirely upon the nature of the bottom. The bays and creeks in the immediate vicinity of any place where a stream enters are generally good ground, as the stream brings down mud and vegetable matter, which, being deposited in the neighbourhood, is peculiarly favourable to the development of insect life. It is by no means uncommon to find the trout in one part of a loch quite red in the flesh, and in another quite white, the red-fleshed ones being on a superior feeding-bank. Sport may almost always be depended upon in the neighbourhood of weeds and large stones, which afford shelter to the trout. The angler should allow his boat to drift alongside, and cast as near to the weeds and stones as possible. Places where the water is overhung with trees should also be fished with great care, as some trout are generally on the outlook for any insects that may drop or be blown from them.

The best trout taken with the fly are usually got in from four to ten feet of water. In the deep parts of the loch little can be done, we believe, because there are few trout in them, the aquatic insects on which they feed being mostly found about the edges, where the sun's rays penetrate to the bottom. Even supposing there were plenty of trout in deep water, unless they should be swimming about near the surface, they could not see the angler's flies; so that fishing in deep water will never prove remunerative.

The opinion prevails that it is of no use angling in lochs unless there is a strong breeze; and if the same size of flies is used always—whether the waters are lashed into foam, or gently agitated, or dead calm—this is quite true. But by adapting the flies and tackle to the circumstances of the case very good sport may be had when there is the slightest breeze, and something may even be done when there is not a ripple on the water. In a calm a long rod and line should be used, in order to get the flies as far away from the boat as possible, as the sight and motion of the boat will alarm the trout in the immediate neighbourhood. When there is no breeze, after the flies light they should be allowed to remain where they are until the motion of their falling has subsided, and then drawn by short jerks towards the angler, more rapidly than if there was a breeze of wind. A larger portion of the line should also be kept in the water, and great care taken to make as little disturbance as possible. Perhaps the best way of fishing in a calm is to have the boat slowly propelled by one oar from the stern, making as little disturbance as possible, and throw gently over every trout that rises at the natural fly. Or if the trout are evidently—as they sometimes are—rising in shoals, the boat may be pulled into the centre of the shoal; and when the alarm caused by the disturbance has subsided and the trout begin to rise again, the angler should drop a small fly lightly on the spot, and he will have a good chance of securing the fish.

The most favourable weather is a day with a good breeze of west wind, and alternate sunshine and shower. The trout never take readily, particularly if the air is at all cold, unless the sun is shining. A wet day is better than a cloudy one without rain, but not equal to a sunny one. In the early months east wind will mar the angler's sport, but in July and August it is not so objectionable; since at that season, even with it, the air is generally sufficiently warm.

The best time of year for fly-fishing depends, as in rivers, upon the season. If the weather is mild, trout may be taken readily in May; but this is rarely the case, and June and July may be set down as the best two months of the year.* In August the trout will not rise so readily, but will take again in September and the beginning of October; but

* Mr. Stewart, from further experience, would probably have admitted that, if this statement can be taken as a rule at all, it must be taken with many exceptions. In some lochs —notably, St. Mary's, Loch Ard, Loch Vennachar—the best of the angling is over in or before May.

fly-fishing in the fall of the season can hardly be called sport, as the trout do not begin to take, after having stopped, till they are in declining condition.

The best time of day depends entirely upon the weather, and it is impossible to name any time with certainty, as the trout may change their humour with every change in the sky. In May the forenoon will generally be found the best; but in June and July from seven in the morning till noon, and again the afternoon from three to five, are the most favourable times. If the weather is very warm, as it sometimes is in July, and there is no wind, about sunset, and an hour or two after it, will be found worth all the rest of the day.

Angling in Loch Leven has come very much into fashion of late years. For some time it was supposed, upon what grounds we are not aware, that the trout of that loch would not rise freely to the artificial fly. This, however, has been found a mistake; they rise just as readily as the trout of any other loch, and there are few lochs so well stocked, and certainly none that contain trout of finer quality. We believe that loch contains more trout for its size than any other loch in Scotland, which is entirely attributable to the great extent of its feeding-ground; the greater part of it being of the depth of from six to twelve feet; just the depth of water best suited to breeding fish. The fishing is under the management of a tacksman, who keeps a number of boats which are let out at half-a-crown an hour, including a man to manage the boat, and, considering that the trout sell at eighteenpence a pound, that two can fish from a boat, and that anglers are allowed to keep their fish, we think the charge moderate. Any of the flies we have recommended for loch-fishing will suit Loch Leven; we have also had very good sport by trolling with Brown's artificial minnow.

The artificial fly is by far the most agreeable and sportsmanlike method of capturing trout in lochs, but is liable to this objection, that the large trout are very rarely taken by it. And though the reader may hear of five, six, and even eight pound trout being taken by this means, he may rest assured that, however well he may fish, he will catch but few such.

The large trout in lochs seem to live principally on their smaller neighbours, and can be more readily taken by trolling than by any other means. It is not at all uncommon to find the trout captured with fly rarely exceeding half-a-pound in weight; while trout of five, ten, and sometimes even twenty pounds' weight, may be taken by means of a small fish for a bait. If the trout are not large, a minnow or parr-tail will form the best bait; but if the angler expects to meet with trout exceeding two or three pounds in weight, a whole parr should be used, and it is superior to a trout, being much more silvery and easily seen. If parr are not procurable, recourse must be had to trout, and if, as is generally the case, they are very dark-coloured when caught, putting them in a white basin and exposing them to the sun will improve their appearance. Where the trout are very large, as in lochs frequented by the *Salmo ferox*, a quarter of a pound trout will not make too large a bait.

The rod for trolling need not be long, but it is absolutely necessary that it should be stiff, as a quantity of line with a heavy fish at the end of it is a severe strain upon a rod, and in such circumstances a supple one would be quite unmanageable. The reel should be large enough to contain at least sixty or seventy yards of good strong line, as a trout of ten or fifteen pounds will make a desperate struggle, and test severely both the skill of the angler and the boatman. After the ordinary line there should be a strong triple-gut casting-line, tapered from the line to where the trolling-tackle is attached. The gut on which the hooks are tied should be stronger than what is used for any other trouting purpose, and almost as thick as that used for salmon-fishing. This strong gut is so rarely devoid of a white glossy appearance, and requires to be stained so dark before it is divested of it, that we prefer triple-gut twisted, which can be got very fine, and it is not so easily seen as a single thread of the same thickness. If there are pike in the loch it will be necessary to tie the hooks on gimp, as the teeth of that fish are very sharp, and will sometimes bite through triple-gut. Two lengths above the hooks a large swivel should be placed, and three or four lengths farther up it is advisable to have a second. Large swivels are greatly superior to small ones, as they are not so liable to go wrong, and also act as sinkers. When sinkers are required, swan-shot should be used, which may be placed between the swivels, or above them.

The number of hooks of which trolling-tackles are composed is very various, and we have seen as many as seven pairs on one tackle. But it is very doubtful if any advantage is gained by surrounding the bait with hooks in this manner, and we think that three, or if the bait is a large one at most four, pairs will be quite sufficient. The hooks should be tied with good strong silk to the same piece of gut, regulating the distance between each pair to suit the length of bait to be used. One of the hooks of the lowermost pair should be stuck into the bait a little above the tail, one of the second pair about the middle, and one of the third pair through the lips. One of the hooks of each pair is thus hidden in the fish, and the other left exposed. The bait must be sufficiently curved to make it spin.

Another kind of trolling-tackle is made in the same manner as the common minnow tackle, but with much larger hooks. The lowermost hook should not be less than from two and a half to three inches long. Fastened to the upper hook is a separate piece of gut, on which are two pairs of hooks, one of which is stuck into the bait about the middle, and the other left loose as a drag, a little beyond the tail. The method of baiting this is the same as that of baiting a minnow, and when the trout or parr is soft from being kept, it has its advantages, as the large hook through the bait keeps it in position.

The best method of trolling is to place the rods in the stern of the boat, with at least twenty yards of line out, so as to keep the bait a good distance from the boat. The latter is then pulled along at a pretty smart pace, and its rising to the waves will play the bait quite as invitingly as the angler could do by hand. A sufficient number of shot should be used to keep the bait two or three feet under the surface, as it is there more likely to attract attention, and the light being less, the character of the lure is not so easily discerned.

The notion that the boat must be pulled against the wind, common among the boatmen, and to which they adhere so tenaciously, is erroneous, but it would be difficult to make a Highland boatman believe this. The error arises from the supposition that the wind is driving the water in the direction it is blowing, whereas it is merely the form of the wave that is going forward, and the bait will spin just as well if the boat is rowed in any direction which is most convenient; either directly with the wind or sideways to it. When the wind is very strong, it is almost impossible to row the boat sufficiently fast against it to keep the bait spinning.

Trolling should be done in deeper water than fly-fishing, and every part of the loch may be trolled over, avoiding the very deep portions. Water from ten to twenty feet deep is usually considered the best ground, but stray fish, and those generally of large size, may be taken even in the middle of the loch.

A dark stormy day is considered most favourable, but no day is objectionable, and even in a dead calm trout may be taken with a small natural or artificial minnow, when they cannot be taken by any other means. In the early part of the season trout will take most freely during the forenoon; but in June and July, if the weather is at all warm, early morning is the best time, and when there is no wind, from sunrise to sunset is the only time when there is much chance of sport by this means. Large fish are most inclined to take when the waters of the loch are high and dark-coloured after a flood.

Trolling is dull work, as it is by no means uncommon for an angler to toil a whole day without getting a single specimen, and even when successful the merit of the capture lies partly with the boatman, who knows the places and rows the boat. Unless the loch is too stormy to fish with fly, we would never advise any one to devote himself to trolling exclusively, but when on the loch it is as well to be provided with a trolling rod and tackle, and to use it when rowing from one place to another, thus filling up the intervals during which he cannot use the fly.

We now come to the last and least interesting method of capturing trout in lochs—namely, with the worm; and on this point we shall be very brief, as it possesses few attractions.

Angling with.the worm can be most successfully practised from the shore, but the angler will require to wade, and a long rod and line are necessary to reach the places where the trout lie. A No. 3 hook is a very good size, and a pretty large black-headed worm should be used. The places frequented by the fly-fisher are also those where the worm-fisher will meet with most sport, and he, like the fly-fisher, is the better of a breeze of wind. After throwing out the worm, it should not be allowed to lie at the bottom, as in that position it is not likely to attract observation, but should be drawn gently along the ground. The best months are June and July, and the morning is the best time of day.

When any river which enters the loch is in full flood good trout may be captured with the worm. The use of a boat is advisable, and the angler should row it round immediately outside of the place where the muddy water becomes mixed with that of the loch, and throwing his bait into the stream, allow it to come towards him. Numbers of good trout may be taken in this way, as they congregate about the mouth of the stream to get the food which it brings down.

CHAPTER XI.

APPLICATION.

WE have treated at considerable length of the four principal methods usually employed for capturing trout. The reader may perhaps be disappointed that salmon-roe fishing has not been added as a fifth ; but our reason for keeping it out is, that we do not consider it a justifiable method of angling, the high price the roe brings affording great, indeed the principal, encouragement to the wholesale destruction of breeding salmon which goes on in Tweed and its tributaries during close time. We think that in the first Act introduced upon the subject of the salmon-fisheries, there should be a clause inserted rendering it illegal for any one to fish with salmon roe, or to be found with it in his possession. Doing away with this traffic would do more to protect the Tweed than all the water-bailiffs between Tweedsmuir and Berwick. There are certainly a few salmon taken shortly before the fishings close, with roe sufficiently matured for curing; but the roe, legally obtained in this way, is not a hundredth part of that taken illegally during close time. Moreover, the fact of salmon being caught in this state in the open season proves that the rivers are open too long, and that the law should be altered in this respect also.

At certain seasons roe is certainly a murderous bait, and a practised roe-fisher might almost depopulate a stream; but then it is only deadly in the fall of the year, when trout are out of condition, or in the spring before they come into it; and killing trout in such circumstances deserves no better name than butchery. For some time roe was, and is still to the north of the Forth, considered an infallible specific for catching trout; a reserve which is to be brought to the attack when everything else fails. It is not, however, looked upon with quite so much favour now. Anglers have begun to find that the presence of a pot of roe in their baskets when setting out by no means ensures the presence of trout there on their return; and we have seen anglers, starting for a first trial of this wonderful bait, sit down at a pool, and, wrapping their plaids about them, remain there for hours, no doubt expecting, according to the common notion, that they would attract all the trout in the neighbourhood, and quite astonished when they had to return without a single one. The fact is, that the wonderful properties of this bait are greatly exaggerated; as a lure for trout during the season when they are in condition it has no advantage, in any state of water, over the lures which have been treated of, and in clear water, during the day, it is almost useless. Nor is the sport, if sport it can be called, by any means attractive; and the practice is so simple as to render it quite unworthy of the attention of the sportsman.

That trout can detect the presence of roe in their neighbourhood is certain; but, in our opinion, the distance at which it is supposed they can do so is greatly exaggerated. Mr. Stoddart mentioned that on several occasions he captured trout which he had every reason to believe had been attracted for half-a-mile by the scent of this bait, which is certainly giving trout credit for possessing extraordinary powers of smell. We think that on the occasions alluded to by Mr. Stoddart, he captured the trout which belonged to a part of the river so much below where he was, not because they had been attracted all that distance by the smell of the roe, but because, when a flood begins to subside in the fall of the year, they travel upwards in search of spawning-ground. As a proof of this, let any one commence angling with the roe in a favourable state of the water during March or April, when trout will take it as readily as in November. On his first commencement at the top of a pool, which we shall suppose is a hundred yards long, he may capture in an hour three or four dozen of trout; but then there comes a stop, and though he were to fish all day in the same place he would get very few more. Let him transfer his operations to the foot of the pool, and he may capture as many more, showing either that the trout cannot detect the presence of roe a hundred yards above them, or that they cannot be troubled to go so far for it, and as they take it as readily in April as November, there is no reason why they should not go as far to seek it in the one month as the other. Another point—which the framers of the next bill upon the salmon-fisheries should keep prominently in view— is the protection of the young salmon or parr. During the months of April and May, when they are changing into smelts and migrating to the sea, killing them is an offence liable to heavy fines; but for the rest of the season, the poor silly parr is at the mercy of every boy who can muster twopence to buy gut and hooks; and thousands of them are slaughtered in Tweed every day during summer, and not by boys only, but by grown men pretending to be anglers. If such have not sufficient skill to capture trout, we hope the law will step in to prevent them massacring the innocents in this manner.*

* Since we wrote the above passage, both roe-fishing and killing parr have been made illegal; but as we believe both are still carried on, if not so openly, nearly as destructively as ever, we have allowed the passage to stand, and hope all

In the first chapter of this volume it was mentioned that there were not three days from May till October in which a good angler should not kill at least twelve pounds weight of trout in any county in the south of Scotland. There are days when he may easily kill twice that quantity, and the angler who, fishing a whole day—that is to say, for nine or ten hours—cannot capture on an average fifteen pounds a day, has not yet attained to eminence in the art. Most anglers seem to think that the difficulty will be to kill the required quantity when the water is clear, but this is not the case, the difficulty is only when the water is flooded. Sport in clear water is certain; sport in flooded water is uncertain. There are occasions when the water is flooded that trout take very readily, and when large baskets may be got with little trouble by almost any one; but these occasions are "like angels' visits, short and far between," and it has not been our lot to fall in with many of them. Indeed, we have frequently, in a dark water, had great difficulty in killing twelve pounds weight, when we could with ease have killed twice that quantity had the water been small and clear; and all our best takes have been when the water was in that condition. There are some days, however, even in clear water, when the most skilful angler will

honest anglers will set their faces against such a disgraceful infringement, not only of the law, but of fair fishing, and not bring discredit upon the fair fame of the craft.

require to work very hard to get the required quantity. Nor is it at all possible to accomplish it by a continuous use of any one method of angling. The fly-fisher cannot do it; the worm-fisher cannot do it; the minnow-fisher cannot do it; and, as a matter of course, the May-fly-fisher cannot do it. It can only be done by a judicious use of the four methods, according to circumstances. Nor can it be done by fishing continually in one stream; the stream also must be varied according to circumstances.

In order to fulfil the promise made to the reader of explaining how this can be done, we shall now go over the whole angling season, and mention the occasions when the angler wishing weight should employ the different methods; but before doing so we shall mention some points which apply equally to all seasons.

One of these is, that large rivers are not so much to be depended upon as small streams, partly because they do not contain so many trout in proportion to their size, and partly because, from unknown causes, the trout in them are more capricious. In the time of a take, large quantities of trout may be caught in them with very little trouble; but at other times the angler will have great difficulty—and will occasionally find it impossible—to kill the required twelve pounds. For this reason, if the angler is not meeting with success in large rivers, he should have recourse to the smaller rivers and waters, and failing these to burns, in which some trout may always be had. We shall suppose that the angler keeps this in view throughout the season, so that it will be unnecessary to make any further allusion to it.

Fishing can be most successfully practised alone; but if the angler fishes in company, he should come to some arrangement with his friend respecting a division of the water before starting, as he who fishes the water first has undoubtedly the best chance. In a large river, and fishing with the fly, it does not make much difference; and even in a small water the trout will rise freely if allowed to remain undisturbed for an hour or so. But it is different in fishing small clear streams with the worm; there the second angler has not nearly so good a chance as his predecessor, and with the minnow or the May-fly, the first angler would entirely mar the sport of the one following him.

Another point equally suitable to all seasons is, if you have got an unlimited stretch of water to fish, to do so very quickly, only taking the best casts. This is peculiarly applicable when the trout are not taking freely. The secret of success lies, to a considerable extent, in getting over the ground rapidly, and the angler who stands casting repeatedly in a spot when he is getting nothing need never expect to fill his basket.

Before trout come into condition there is no inducement to fish for them; and not being in the streams, no reliance can be placed upon their taking; and as they are rarely in condition all over a county till the first of May, we shall begin with that month. Should trout come into condition sooner, the lures suitable for May will be found suitable for April also.

In the beginning of May it is of little use starting before eight o'clock in the morning, as the weather is generally cold; if the weather is warm, however, trout will take an hour or two earlier. When the waters are clear the angler should commence with the creeper, and continue using it till he sees the take has commenced, when he should at once change to the fly, and make the most of his time. At this season the take lasts longer than at any other, and if the day is favourable, the angler may kill the required quantity in a few hours in the forenoon. During the afternoon— that is to say, from two or three o'clock till six or seven—the minnow will frequently be found the best; and a very good plan is to fish up with the creeper and fly, and then back over the same ground with the minnow. If neither the creeper, fly, nor minnow will take, recourse must be had to the worm; but this is rarely the case, and unless on the occasion of a full flood, the angler may never have occasion to use the worm till the end of June. When the waters are in full flood recourse must be had to the worm; and when they are rising or again falling, from the time that the particles of the mud begin to subside until the waters become of a dark porter colour, the minnow will be found very deadly. The worm and the minnow should be used the whole season through when the waters are in the state just mentioned, but when they become of a dark porter colour the lures appropriate to the season come into play; and in May, in such a case, reliance can always be placed upon the fly.

About the middle of the month the May-fly makes its appearance, and with it the angler will have no difficulty in filling his basket. In streams where the May-fly is not to be had, the angler should use worm and minnow in the morning, and whenever he observes the trout rising at the natural insect change to the fly. The minnow will again be found effective in the evening. Even in streams where May-flies abound, minnow or worm will sometimes take better than they do early in the morning, and if the weather is very dark and stormy, the minnow will frequently be found most effective all day.

When the May-flies have been two or three weeks on the water, or about the middle of June, they are not to be found in such numbers; the trout also do not take them so readily; and filling even a twelve-pound basket becomes rather difficult. The trout have given up taking fly readily, and have not yet begun to take worm; they appear to be resting after the high feeding they have enjoyed for the last six weeks. Loch-fishing being now in its prime, the angler would do well to give it a trial, as he will not lose much by a ten days' absence from the rivers. In these the worm and minnow in the morning, the fly in the forenoon, and the minnow and fly in the evening, will be found the best means of filling a basket; and in small waters and hill-burns trout will now take the worm readily.

From the middle to the end of June worm-fishing commences, and from this period to the end of July large basketsful of trout may be depended upon, no matter what the state of weather or water. A good arrangement for a day's trouting at this season is to start very early in the morning —the earlier the better—and fish down a few miles with the minnow, and then fish back again with the worm; or, if the angler has not the gift of early rising, he may start about breakfast-time, taking his dinner with him, and fish up with the worm and down again with the minnow in the evening.

About the beginning of August another change begins to take place in the inclinations of the trout. Unless the weather is showery, or particularly favourable, they will not take the worm readily; and frequently only take it for an hour or so in the heat of the day. There is also a visible falling off in the size of the trout caught with it —a sure sign with any kind of fishing that it is approaching a termination. Nor will the minnow, unless the streams are swollen, aid the angler in his emergency; there is nothing for it but to have recourse to the more backward districts and smaller waters.

About the end of August trout begin to take the fly freely, and continue doing so all through September, and reliance can generally be placed upon it, particularly in coloured water; should it fail, recourse must be had to some hill-burn, where the worm will always be found effective.

By the beginning of October all the spawning trout are out of condition; the small ones, however, which do not spawn, afford very good diversion until far on in the month, by which time even they are quite unworthy the attention of the sportsman; affording no play when hooked, and no satisfaction when caught. In other respects also angling is divested of half its charms; there is nothing cheering, nothing invigorating, in a ramble by a river's side. The angler's path is not now adorned with the daisy and the violet, or scented with the perfume of innumerable wild flowers; and the singing of the birds, and the hum of the mountain-bee are replaced by the sighing of the wind among leafless branches, or along a bleak hill-side. Nature is fast resuming her wintry aspect, and

> "When chill November's surly blast
> Makes fields and forests bare,"

END OF THE ANGLING SEASON.

the angler who has followed his vocation in the joyous spring-time, and again when the summer's sun throws his rich glories over mountain and valley; and has continued with undiminished ardour when the breezes play cooler,

> "And Autumn's soberer hues
> Tint the ripe fruit, and gild the waving corn,"

will not lose much by bidding adieu to the streams for the season, and awaiting, with thankfulness for the past and bright hopes for the future, the coming of another spring.

INDEX.

AGRICULTURAL drainage, xxxii, 24
Angling fables, 9 *et seq.*
Aquatic insects, 24 *et seq.*
Atmospheric influences, 130

BAILLIE, James, xxiv, 59
Baskets, 52
Breeze, favourable, 116, 204

CAST of flies, 97 *et seq.*, 119
Casting, 104
Creeper, the, 165

DOWN-STREAM casting, 69
Dress, 33

FAVOURITE streams, 17
Feeding in various waters, 17 *et seq.*
Flies, xxxix *et seq.*, 76 *et seq.*; colour of, 81; light dressing, 85; gutta-percha wings, 86; hackles of, 86; favourite wings, 87, 89; sizes of, 118; positions on cast, 120; hatch of, 122; for lochs, 195 *et seq.*

Fly-dressing instruments, 90
Fly-fishing, 55 *et seq.*
Francis Francis, Mr., 82

GALA WATER, 30
Grilse, 25
Gut, 44, 79, 200, 208

HIGHLAND lochs, xxxviii, 193
Hooks, 48 *et seq.*

LANDING-net, 52
Lines, 43
Loch-fishing, 192 *et seq.*
Loch Leven, 206

MAGGOT, the, 130
Malloch, Mr P. D., xxxix
March brown, the, 122
May a good month, 125
May-fly, the, xxxiv, 78, 163 *et seq.*
Minnow and parr-tail, 173 *et seq.*
Minnow-tackle, 180 *et seq.*, 209
Minnows, traps for, 176
Muir, Mr. William, 194

NETTING, methods of prevention, 28
Night-fishing, 129

POCKET-BOOK, 53
Pollution, 25

REELS, 42
Rods, xxxv, 35 *et seq.*, 100, 201

SALMON in trout-streams, 20
Salmon-roe, 214
Spawning accommodation, 19
Spinners, spiders, xl, 85, 88, 91, 127, 129
Stoddart, Mr., 60, 216
Stone-fly, the, 126, 164
Streams in south of Scotland, 11

Striking, 108
Superstition, a Highland, 210

"TIME of the take," 123
Trolling, 207 *et seq.*
Trout, qualities of, 7 *et seq.*; senses of, 13 *et seq.*; season of condition, 22; decrease of, 23
Tweed, the, 18, 24; *Quarterly Review* on, 26

UP-STREAM casting, 63 *et seq.*

WILSON, Mr., 164
Wind, the, 205
Worm-fishing, 60, 134 *et seq.*; best time for, 223
Worms, varieties of, 143 *et seq.*

INTRODUCTION TO "A CAUTION TO ANGLERS."

Disagreement, dispute and debate are features of angling in all eras but the small booklet *A Caution to Anglers or 'The Practical Angler' and the 'Modern Practical Angler' Compared* is about as outspoken and acidic as such exchanges get without formal legal action. Couched in the nominally courteous tones of Victorian sportsmen, the correspondence between the careful, serious and indignant Scot and the rather bemused but belligerent and unrepentant Mr Pennell is still entertaining.

Although Stewart contends the debate began as a result of Cholmondeley Pennell's refusal to re-name or withdraw what William C. regarded as his deliberately confusingly named book *The Modern Practical Angler*, the nub of their acrimonious exchange, which was conducted in the pages of *The Field* magazine, was their fundamentally different approach to fishing for trout.

The carefully considered and finely crafted Stewart summary of the wisdom of using appropriately coloured and sparsely dressed 'spiders' fished upstream was summarily dismissed and contradicted by the old-fashioned Cholmondeley Pennell in his 'modern' wide ranging work. Clearly irked and insulted the young Scot was in no mood to back down and in the columns of *The Field* battle was publicly joined.

As Arthur Ransome so ably put it,
"*A Caution to Anglers*, a pamphlet of embittered argument between the two of them in which there are accusations of plagiary, of lying and even of bad fishing. Well, they have both been long dead and, I suppose, fish the Styx, one fishing up and one fishing down and pass each other without speaking. Stewart's is the better book and the better advice but Pennell's is also worth reading."

In later works, following Stewart's death, Cholmondeley Pennell continued to re-visit the argument relying largely upon the approach that because Stewart's experience was particularly Scottish his theories were therefore not valid in England. The anglers of that realm should instead look towards a certain Cholmondeley Pennell for advice.

He also stated "Poor Stewart! He was a fine fisherman and a right good companion, and pleasant days we fly-fished side by side, ..."
In the light of their Loch Leven encounter and the contents of their correspondence it seems more than a little optimistic to propose that the thoughtful William Stewart would have echoed those sentiments.
Although time has vindicated Stewart's view, and

Cholmondelely Pennell's have more recently been described as "tosh", perhaps the last words properly belong to the editor of *The Field* who in 1871, despite feeling obliged to bring the conflict to a premature public conclusion, reviewed *A Caution* in the following terms:

"Mr Stewart is clearly a good, honest, thorough fighter; he asks no quarter and he gives none. Most of our readers remember the passage of arms between those doughty antagonists Mr Stewart of *The Practical Angler* fame and Mr C. Pennell of *The Modern Practical Angler*. Mr Stewart seems to have been dissatisfied with his opponent's riding off and claiming a victory, when in his view of the case, and that of many others, "the boot was clean on the other leg."

On Stewart's death a few months later the editor, Francis Francis wrote "Mr Stewart was known personally to us …a better angler or kindlier has rarely trod the bank of any river".

Richard Hunter

Perth, March 2009

A

CAUTION TO ANGLERS

OR

'THE PRACTICAL ANGLER'

AND 'THE MODERN PRACTICAL ANGLER'

COMPARED

WITH

REMARKS UPON THE DECREASE OF TROUT

AND PROPOSED REMEDIES

BY W. C. STEWART

AUTHOR OF 'THE PRACTICAL ANGLER'

EDINBURGH

ADAM AND CHARLES BLACK

1871

PREFACE.

THAT Mr. Pennell should write a book, whether he had any information to impart or not, is a matter of which no one can complain. That he should call that book, however, by a title so similar to mine, my publishers complained of to his, and requested them to alter it, as the similarity or title might lead to purchasers getting the one book when they wished the other. As they declined to do this, and I am afraid that, in spite of the discovery of a previous *Practical Angler*, any confusion in this way might be chiefly detrimental to *The Practical Angler* which goes by my name, I publish this pamphlet—portions of which have already appeared in the *Field*—to show that the similarity is almost entirely confined to the title, and that no two systems of fly-fishing could be more different than those advocated in *The Practical Angler*, and *The Modern Practical Angler*.

I am further stimulated to what is somewhat an ungracious task, by not having seen any review of *The Modern Practical Angler*, which thoroughly tears to tatters the web of absurdities in which Mr. Pennell has involved himself; most reviewers giving them the go-by lightly. The *Scotsman*, indeed, remarked that Mr. Pennell might safely be left to the mercy of his own arguments, and if all his readers were thoroughly qualified anglers it would be difficult to imagine a severer punishment; but as more of the readers of angling works are learners than proficients, and as they cannot so readily distinguish between the genuine and the counterfeit, I propose for their benefit criticising the system of fly-fishing and flies which its author expects to "revolutionise fly-fishing," and "write the epitaph of the present system of artificial flies."

I have also some grounds of complaint against *The Modern Practical Angler*, which will be fully stated in the following pages, and upon which I court the opinion of the angling community.

EDINBURGH, *27th March* 1871.

A CAUTION TO ANGLERS.

LETTERS TO THE EDITOR OF THE FIELD.

MODERN AND ANCIENT (?) PRACTICAL ANGLERS.

SIR—In your paper of the 17th ult. I notice a letter from Mr. H. Cholmondeley-Pennell, in which he backs up the views of fly-fishing down stream which he has advocated in his book, *The Modern Practical Angler*. As Mr. Pennell has alluded to me frequently in his book, and almost entirely in his letter, as an exponent of up-stream fishing, perhaps you will allow me space to say something in reply to his letter, and also to make a few remarks upon his book. First, then, for the letter. In it Mr. Pennell says the arguments in favour of up-stream fishing are:—

"1. That, as trout always lie head up stream, the angler fishing from below is less likely to be seen than one fishing from above."

"*Answer.*— The position of the eye of a trout is such as to enable him to see much more readily anything above or on one side than in front of him; and in rippling water, such as trout streams usually consist of, the angler making moderately long casts will, for all practical purposes, be out of 'ken' of the fish, whether he stands above or below."

If Mr. Pennell in his rather vague answer means that trout see as well behind as in front, why does he in his book instruct anglers to throw a foot above a rising fish? why not throw a foot behind him? If Mr. Pennell admits, what every angler knows to be a fact, that trout see better in front than behind—nature having formed them for looking out for their food the way it comes, down stream—why does he attempt to answer the argument at all?

"2. That the angler striking from below is likely to strike the hook into the fish's jaws, whereas the angler striking from above is likely to 'pull the flies straight out of his mouth.' "

"*Answer.*—This is true as an abstract proposition, but as applied to the question of fly-fishing up stream is quite untrue. When the fly is being drawn straight down stream, the trout, rising from below, is forced, owing to the position of the gut, *to turn round before he can take the fly*; so that at the moment of rising the fish would be in precisely the same position with regard to the angler, whether the latter was fishing up or down."

In answer to Mr. Pennell's answer, it may be

pointed out that an up-stream fisher never draws his flies at all, but allows them to float down as the natural insect does; also, that he very rarely casts directly above him, but generally up and across. Mr. Pennell says (upon what grounds it is difficult even to imagine) that "the position of the gut compels the trout to turn round before he can take the fly." That is, that the trout sees the fly coming down stream, but also sees the gut is in his way so he either bolts up stream or waits till the fly passes him, and then turns round with his head down stream and catches it. It is by no means clear why the gut should be more in the trout's way in the one position than the other; but most anglers will be of opinion that if the trout saw the gut he would not put himself to so much trouble to take the fly. Had Mr. Pennell stated that trout turned a summersault or two before taking the fly, it would be quite as probable in theory and correct in fact.

Mr. Pennell's answer to the third argument will be fully replied to subsequently, in taking notice of his flies and system of fishing.

Mr. Pennell in his letter adds: —

"Even, therefore, if it could be proved that some-what more fish were to be taken by fishing up than down stream, anglers might well hesitate before they adopted the system. My own experience, however, leads to an opposite conclusion, and it is an experience corroborated, as I believe, by that of the great majority of anglers. Indeed, Mr. Stewart him-self practically admits this when he states that 'ninety-nine anglers out of a hundred fish down;' and in a subsequent (fourth) edition that, notwithstanding what he has written, 'fishing up stream with the fly has not been adopted by a large portion of the angling community.'

"I do not doubt that Mr. Pennell and the majority of anglers may catch more fish fishing down than up probably for the reason mentioned at page 67 of the fifth edition of *The Practical Angler*, which, as all your readers may not have a copy beside them, I will quote:—

"Fishing up is *much more* difficult than fishing down, requiring more practice, and a better acquaintance with the habits of the trout; and we believe that a mere novice would, on a large water, catch more trout by fishing down than up, because the latter *requires more nicety in casting*; but to attain anything like eminence in fly-fishing the angler must fish up," etc.

Mr. Pennell says that I practically admit the benefit of down-stream fishing when I say that ninety-nine anglers out of a hundred fish down. I published *The Practical Angler* thirteen years ago for the sole purpose of showing that the *ninety-nine anglers fished wrong*; and how Mr. Pennell can so distort my statements and misrepresent my ideas as to say that I "practically admit to be right" what I spent weeks in labouring to prove wrong, I cannot understand. The unblushing coolness of the statement is enough to take away one's breath. Mr. Pennell continues:— "And in a subsequent (fourth) edition, that, notwithstanding what he has written, fishing up stream with the fly has not been adopted by a large portion of the angling community." Picking out a few lines here and there, without giving the context, is not the fairest way of representing a question; and if Mr. Pennell intended quoting the passage at all, he should have finished it. It is too lengthy to give here, but the reader will find it in pages 67 to 71 of *The Practical Angler*. The number of up-stream fishers, however, has greatly increased of late years, as you are no doubt aware; and they will continue to increase, in spite of Mr. Pennell's backsliding to the old system.

Although I think I have reason to complain of some things in Mr. Pennell's book, I should never have thought of writing to any newspaper upon the subject had I not been attacked; having been attacked, however, I suppose I may be "permitted to speak for myself," and if in doing so I require to make more reference to *The Practical Angler* than I like, I hope your readers will excuse me. I offer no excuse to Mr. Pennell for making remarks upon his book, because it is a volume with very considerable pretensions, and his writing again shows that he courts rather than shuns criticism.

The first subject which Mr. Pennell lays much stress upon is the form of hook a subject which he correctly considers of great importance and introduces what he calls the Pennell hook, "the result of some thought and experiment." If your readers will compare pages 7 to 10 of *The Modern Practical Angler* with pages 47 and 48 of *The Practical Angler*, I think they will be forced to the conclusion that Mr. Pennell's hook need not have cost him any thought or experiment. The illustrations and reasoning in both cases are almost identical, the only difference being, that he has made the turn of the hook at a more acute angle, rendering it more liable to break, and the barb of the hook longer, rendering it more difficult to fix.

Mr. Pennell's system of flies and fly-fishing, how- ever, is what he prides himself upon, and but for it his "book would certainly not have been written." Upon these points there is something both new and old; the flies are new with a vengeance; the system is a return to the ancient. Fly-fishers he divides into two classes, formalists and colourists, which he pits against each other, and then pitches into each by turns. By the formalists Mr. Pennell seems to mean the school so ably represented by Mr. Francis Francis, who believe that an exact imitation of the fly on the water will prove more killing than any other. This school may very well be left to answer Mr. Pennell for themselves. It is not quite so easy to know what he means by the "colourists." The following is his reply of the "colourists" to the "formalists":—

"Your theory supposes that trout can detect the nicest shades of distinction between specimens of flies which on a summer's afternoon may be numbered actually by hundreds, thus crediting them with an amount of entomological knowledge which even a professed naturalist, to say nothing of the angler him-self, rarely possesses; whilst at the same time you draw your flies up and across stream in a way in which no natural insect is ever seen, not only adding to the impossibility of discriminating between different species, but often rendering it difficult for the fish to identify the flies as flies. The only thing a fish can distinguish under these circumstances, besides the size of fly, is its colour. We therefore regard form as a matter of comparative indifference, and colour as all-important."

As the first part of this extract is almost word for word the same as *The Practical Angler*, I am entitled to suppose that Mr. Pennell classes me as a colourist. The last two sentences of the passage quoted are Mr. Pennell's own; how far they agree with *The Practical Angler* the following quotation will show:—

"We must now consider what it is necessary to imitate, or what do trout take, or rather mistake, the artificial fly for. As before stated, we believe that, deceived by an appearance of life, they take it for what it is intended to imitate—a fly, or some other aquatic insect. In proof of this, artificial flies are not of much use unless the trout are at the time feeding on the natural insect; and an artificial fly will kill twenty trout for one which the feathers composing it, rolled round the hook without regard to shape, will. Nay, more, a neatly made, natural-looking fly will, where trout are shy, kill three trout for one which a clumsy fly will. . . . The great point, then, in fly-dressing, is to make the artificial fly resemble the natural insect in shape."

Having put, as he expresses it, "both formalists and colourists out of court," Mr. Pennell proceeds to have his innings. Some miscellaneous remarks follow about dry and wet flies, imitating nature, and simulating life; these processes being accomplished as follows:—"It is of the utmost consequence that the fly should be as 'fly-like' and characteristic as possible, so that, notwithstanding its rapid and unnatural movements, *it may be at once and unmistakably identified as a fly.*" Mr. Pennell backs this up by the statement that "ninety-nine men out of a hundred find it best to give a slight movement to the fly in the water." Did it never occur to Mr. Pennell, and the ninety-nine men out of a hundred who, he says, keep him company, that the chances of the said fly being "at once and unmistakably identified as a fly" would be considerably improved by a natural instead of an unnatural movement? Mr. Pennell, be it observed, says men, not anglers. How the men may fish I cannot say, but for the anglers on this side the Tweed (and they are very bad to beat), I have fished with all the best of them, and not one gives any motion to his flies.

There is one point upon which a large number of the very best anglers will agree with Mr. Pennell: that is, "general shape, general colour, and size, are all that can be distinguished by the fish. These are the points, therefore, to be kept in view in the construction of artificial trout-flies." He then proceeds to construct what he calls three typical flies upon these principles, and his method of doing so, or "imitating nature," is profoundly original and thoroughly amusing. "As regards form or shape, no question can arise, as the selected families are all unmistakably and characteristically *flies* in the proper sense of the term, having wings, legs," etc. A little farther on: "The great majority of the most favourite river flies belong to the order Neuroptera, or nerve-winged insects, the wings of which, being filmy and transparent, cannot be really imitated by feathers, or by any other available material. Wings, therefore, are merely an incumbrance to the artificial trout-fly, and should be entirely rejected." Having established, on page 72, that "it is doubly important that the imitation insect should be as characteristic and fly-like as possible," and further established that all flies have wings, Mr. Pennell commences to imitate nature by dispensing with wings altogether. The reader must not suppose, however, that the fly is to be left almost naked. Not at all; this is not the way Mr. Pennell imitates nature. The deficiency thus caused is to be filled up by giving the fly three times the number of legs to which it had a natural right, or what he himself describes (his own words) "as an unnatural quantity of legs."

Having now got a fly as "fly-like as possible," with no wings and an unnatural quantity of legs, he proceeds to the next great desideratum—colour. And here I may remark that, when I reduced the list of artificial flies to six (three winged flies and three spiders), I thought I had done quite enough in that way; but Mr. Pennell, having hit upon the making of flies without wings, has an obvious advantage over me, and reduces them to three, what he calls typical flies, and selects what he says are the three colours most usually predominating in river insects. These colours are first, dark green; second, fiery or cinnamon brown; third, darkish golden olive. If any reader will look at the illustrations of these flies in Mr. Pennell's book, he will at once come to the conclusion that Mr. Pennell has been singularly appropriate in his choice of a name for them, as, not being an imitation of anything at present existing, they must be typical of something to come.

Such are the methods of imitating nature in the construction of flies, and simulating life in the working of them, which are to revolutionise fly-fishing. On coming to some of the passages quoted, a horrid suspicion crossed the writer's mind that Mr. Pennell—who is very fond of a joke—might be in fun; but no, he is evidently terribly in earnest; and if no other person believes in his system, he at least believes in it himself, as the following modest quotation will show:—

"Indeed, when I think now great that ingenuity has been, how much has been written, and charmingly written, for the last two centuries, to teach how to make and use what I have been exhorting my readers to discard as useless; and what a complicated and nicely-balanced system has been thereon elaborated; it is not without a pang of regret I have undertaken the ungracious task of writing what may perhaps eventually prove to be its epitaph."

So much for Mr. Pennell's theory of fly-fishing; and now to take a look at his practice. He says his system, has been "worked out, tested, and re-tested by myself during some twenty years' practical experience of fly-fishing on many of the principal rivers and lakes of the three kingdoms." As a proof of this he writes:—

"Local prejudices are by no means confined to professional fishermen. Even first-rate amateur performers are often imbued with the notion that no flies but those they have been accustomed to consider the correct thing on particular rivers and streams will kill in them. I remember once fishing the most famous trouting loch in Scotland, in company with two of her most celebrated (and justly celebrated) anglers, and when I showed them the flies I meant to use, they assured me that they ' would never kill fish in Lochleven!' At the end of the first day, however, my basket, which included seven trout, weighing 14 lb., was found to be heavier than both theirs."

This passage has been already answered in the *Scotsman* newspaper, but, as all your readers may not see the *Scotsman*, I quote it:—

"We have heard something about that great national overthrow and humiliation. There is evidence extant to the effect that those two luckless amateurs whom Mr. Pennell came to Scotland to put to shame, said, not that his flies would not kill fish, but that they were not so suitable to kill fish at that place as some other flies. Also it is averred that—though it is true that in two or three hours' evening fishing Mr. Pennell, with his miraculous flies, did happen to kill seven large trout, whilst his companions and victims happened to alight on fewer or smaller it is also true that on the next day, which was a much longer and consequently fairer trial, one of the vanquished, with the flies common to the place, did better than Mr. Pennell and the flies in which he puts all his trust, by something like fourfold. Of course this is but a trifling incident; but just for that reason, as well as for another, it cannot, as stated by Mr. Pennell, be admitted as evidence of his theory."

As one of the occupants of the boat on this celebrated occasion, I may be permitted to add that Mr. Pennell who, it is as well to mention, was mostly using winged flies, and not of the typical colour thought his flies very superior, and was assured by me that neither flies nor fishing mattered much on Lochleven, as the very best anglers were frequently disgracefully beaten by parties who had never thrown a fly before.

What Mr. Pennell calls the first day's fishing commenced at 6 P.M., and terminated shortly after 8 P.M., when Mr. Pennell had seven trout, one of his companions six, and the other five. He, how-ever, was fortunate in securing a three-and-a-half-pounder, so that his basket weighed more than either of the others. The wording of the passage, "His basket, which included seven trout," would lead to the supposition that he had other trout besides, which was not the case: seven was the entire take. Now, what I complain of is, that Mr. Pennell should misrepresent the statements of his companions, suppress the fact of there being a second and whole day's fishing in which, as well as on the gross time, he was very much behind one of his companions and proceed upon this to claim superiority for flies, which, if he was using at all, I never saw. Such conduct needs no comment; and if it was only a slip of memory, Mr. Pennell has had plenty of time to put matters right since the above appeared in the *Scotsman*. It may be as well to mention, what the *Scotsman's* reviewer has omitted, that, as we were fishing three in a boat, and Mr. Pennell was a stranger, he had always an end of the boat to him-self; and, as he either could not or would not cast but from his right hand, he was half the time cast-ing over the centre of the boat, thereby considerably lessening the chances of the occupant of that station, who had always to watch his opportunity to cast when Mr. Pennell was not.

The question of up or down stream fly-fishing Mr. Pennell passes over very lightly, merely assuming that the latter is correct the reason, I suppose, that he has attempted to strengthen his position by his answers in *The Field*. As the arguments in favour of up-stream fishing are the same in Mr. Francis's book as in mine, and much more concisely stated, I take the liberty of quoting them:—

"And now a word or two about the much-discussed point as to fishing up stream or down; though what there is to discuss in it, or how any difference of opinion can exist, I am at a loss to understand. The angler should never fish down stream if he can by any possibility fish up. The fish lie with their heads up stream. They see the flies coming down towards them, and they rise to meet them. The angler is far behind them, and of course they are not so likely to see him. If a fish takes the fly fairly, then the angler will, if he strikes properly, hardly ever miss his fish, because he pulls the fly towards, and as it were into, the fish's mouth; whereas in fishing down he will perpetually pull it out of his mouth. Added to this, in fishing down, every fish for twenty yards can see him coming, and the best will cease rising and take shelter under some weed. Again, if he hooks a good fish that requires play, he must take it down over unfished ground, disturbing every fish for some distance, or create much disturbance of the water, and risk breaking the hold on the tackle. . . . But to cast down stream, and work the fly up, is not fly- fishing."

At page 68 of *The Practical Angler* there is the following, alluding to anglers of Mr. Pennell's stamp:—

"As no amount of mere argument will convince such, we offer to find two anglers who, on a water suitable for showing the superiority of fishing up, will be more successful than any three anglers fishing down after the ordinary method."

This passage has remained for thirteen years unchallenged, but has probably escaped Mr. Pennell's notice. However, to bring the matter to a practical test, if he will fish himself under the before-mentioned conditions, and use his typical flies, I will find an angler to fish against him, and will bet a considerable sum of money, to be given to any charity the winner may choose, that the said angler will catch two pounds' weight of trout for his one; and, until the question is put to the proof, it is useless writing more upon the subject.

In his chapter on worm-fishing, Mr. Pennell introduces a new worm-tackle, by reducing the three-hook tackle, which usually goes by my name, to two, and making the hooks a little larger. The following are the reasons, *pro* and *con*, as given in the *Scotsman*:—

"In the first place, he mistakes when he represents that tackle as consisting always of four hooks. Mr. Stewart, we think, once wrote somewhere 'three or four;' but three has been the understood and adopted number for many years. In the second place, when advocating his own plan of two hooks, Mr. Pennell gives five reasons, every one of which admits of being smashed:—(1) 'It is baited in less than half the time' The time cannot possibly be less than half, and, as a good deal of the time employed in the operation, such as taking from the bag and bringing the bait into a proper position, must be employed whether the hooks are two or four, the time saved by omitting two hooks must be quite infinitesimal. (2.) 'The worm lives much longer.' In both cases the worm lives quite long enough for the purpose, and it dies by being drowned, not by being transfixed. (3.) 'Its appearance is much more natural and lively.' Quite the reverse; with 'two hooks the greater proportion of the worm must either be left entirely unarmed, or a large and clumsy 'bulge' or 'slack' must be left between the two hooks, whilst with three hooks the bait can be thrown into any form the angler chooses. (4.) 'The hooks are comparatively unseen.' Again quite the reverse; Mr. Pennell admits that his two hooks must be larger than Mr. Stewart's three, and two large hooks are much more easily detected than three tiny ones. (5.) 'They are 'disgorged' in half the time.' That would be true if in the one case the trout were always caught by two hooks, and in the other by four, which is very rare, and not the common case."

In addition, I may mention that I tested the two hooks thoroughly fourteen years ago, fishing half-hour about with the two hooks and the single hook, and found the latter killed most.

The chapter on Mayfly-fishing, in *The Modern Practical Angler*, is entirely copied from *The Practical Angler*, as your readers may see for themselves by comparison; indeed, in this case so closely has Mr. Pennell stuck to his text, as to raise the suspicion that he is practically unacquainted with what he was writing about, and was afraid to introduce any novelty for fear of "putting his foot in it." Would it be asking too much of Mr. Pennell to let us know how often he fished with the creeper and Mayfly, and what he caught?

By the way, it is rather curious to find Mr. Pennell, who lays considerable claims to ichthyology, and would have every angler be an ichthyologist, making a mistake in the ichthyology of the principal fish he is writing about. The salmon or kipper, he says, "is a male salmon after spawning;" whereas a kipper means merely a male fish, whether clean, foul, or kelted. A baggit, he says, is a female fish just after spawning; whereas a baggit as Mr. Pennell might know from the meaning of the word is a female fish immediately before spawning.

To bring my lengthy, and I am afraid tedious, letter to a conclusion, I have endeavoured as much as possible to confine my remarks to those points on which *The Modern Practical Angler* and *The Practical Angler* are at variance. I mentioned previously that I thought I had some grounds of complaint against Mr. Pennell; these are, to state them briefly, that he has distorted my statements, suppressed facts which were against him, borrowed my ideas and information, and made an appropriate consummation to the whole by borrowing my title. And, not content with that, he prefixes to my original title the word "Modern," thereby conveying the insinuation that mine is ancient—in fact, adding insult to injury. Your readers will probably perceive that I am not pleased with Mr. Pennell; whether "I do well to be angry" or not, I leave you and them to judge, and also the materials on which to form a judgment.

W. C. Stewart.

Edinburgh, *October 1.*

Modern and Ancient Practical Anglers.

Sir—"Tantæne animis cælestibus iræ?" Your excellent correspondent and my very good friend Mr. Stewart is in a passion, and the fact is so patent throughout the three columns of invective which you publish in your last number, that it was almost a labour of love on his part to wind up with a solemn declaration of the fact. As, however, I am not aware that in my book, with which he is so angry, I have ever mentioned his name except in terms of marked (and deservedly marked) eulogy, I am driven to conclude that it must be my matter, and not my manner, that has excited his wrath. In other words, he has paid my arguments the proverbial compliment of losing his temper at them.

Whether he has any other just grounds, or any grounds whatever, for doing so, I will, with your permission, briefly examine, and I shall at once pass to the personal questions at issue between us, though, for my own part, I detest personalities, if for no other reason than that they possess so small a share of interest for the public at large. Mr. Stewart, how-ever, drives me to the *argumentum ad hominem*, and I am reluctantly obliged to follow.

On the original *casus belli*, Up or Down stream fishing, I shall not dwell, as I have nothing to add to the arguments which I adduced on this subject in *The Field* of September 24. Mr. Stewart has now equally fully stated his views; and both having been supplemented and commented upon in a number of able letters from your correspondents, amongst whom I recognised with pleasure so excellent a fisherman and sportsman as Col. Whyte, the question may be said to be fairly before the High Court of Anglers, and they will no doubt be able to form their own judgment on the point. The same observations apply to the theory of trout flies, and how they should be used. If those who care about the subject will look at my book, *The Modern Practical Angler*, they will find the whole question carefully examined, and most of Mr. Stewart's arguments refuted by anticipation.

The first point on which Mr. Stewart falls foul of me personally is the form of hook now manufactured under my name, and which Mr. Stewart says in effect is copied from one recommended in his book. This hook of mine more nearly approaches the sneck than any other kind. On turning to the pages to which he refers in *The Practical Angler*, I find that Mr. Stewart recommends, as the result of his investigations, the ordinary "round-bend" hooks which have been manufactured by Messrs. Bartlett and Addlington for many years, and suggests on his own account *no improvement or modification in them whatever*. Mr. Stewart's hook, which he accuses me of plagiarising, must therefore be pronounced a myth.

Another subject of attack is the title of my book—*The Modern Practiced Angler*—in which Mr. Stewart complains that I have "appropriated" that of his own. Is Mr. Stewart in earnest, or is he perpetrating a little joke to test the angling erudition of the readers of *The Field*? Can he really be ignorant that he has himself actually transferred bodily to the first page of his own volume the exact title of another book published some fifteen years before—*The Practical Angler*, by "Piscator" (Simpkin and Marshall, 1843 and 1846)—and which has subsequently passed through several editions? Further, can Mr. Stewart be unaware that during the last half-century there have been no less than thirteen angling books published, of the titles of which the word "Practical" forms part? But Mr. Stewart has not only plagiarised the title of another author, he has also falsified his own, inasmuch as the term *Practical Angler* implies a treatise on angling generally, whilst his is admittedly only a monograph—a treatise, that is, on *one subject*. I am sorry to be obliged thus to turn the tables on Mr. Stewart, but he has challenged the rejoinder.

Mr. Stewart objects that in my chapter on Creeper and May-fly fishing I have borrowed from him. If any one else, after comparing the two books, should be of the same opinion, I shall be surprised.

I willingly admit my obligations to Mr. Stewart, for many valuable suggestions, both on this and other points; but I fancied that in this instance I had sufficiently acknowledged them, by recommending all anglers to study Mr. Stewart's "excellent chapter on the subject."

Again, as regards his worm-tackle, Mr. Stewart complains that, in contrasting it with my own, I have represented it as consisting of four hooks, when the real number which he recommends is three. In reply, I have only to observe that in his *Practical Angler*, which I have now before me, the illustrative diagram of his worm-tackle shows the number of hooks *as four*, and that I have, when referring to this subject in the *Modern Practical Angler*, actually taken the trouble of *giving a facsimile of the tackle in question*, adding, that "I give Mr. Stewart the greatest credit for the originality of this idea, which belongs to him alone." In the name of common sense, what can Mr. Stewart find here to take exception to? Are not these repeated and specific acknowledgments, with others of a similar character, sufficient to satisfy the most exacting requirements of the most irritable of the *irritabile genus*?

But the greatest stumbling-block of all to Mr. Stewart appears to be the account which I have given of a case in which flies of the colours I advocate for lake fishing—

viz. green and yellow—were found on Lochleven to be more successful than those of two other anglers. I did not, of course, so far violate the canons of courtesy as to mention either of these gentlemen by name, or give any clue by which they could be identified; but, as Mr. Stewart has "put on the cap," I am happy to acknowledge that he was one of the "justly celebrated anglers" referred to in my book as having been on this occasion the victims of local prejudice—a result which I took trouble to emphasise, "I attribute, of course, solely to the flies, not, be it well understood, to the fisherman." My memory of all the circumstances of this "fly-match," if I may so for the moment characterise it, differs materially from Mr. Stewart's on almost every one of the important points to which he alludes; as, for example, the day on which the fishing in question occurred, my remembrance being that we fished on three distinct days, and not two, and that it was on the second or complete day that my creel outweighed his; the number of the trout composing my basket on the day in question; the proportionate weight of Mr. Stewart's basket on the day following, when I do not think either of the takes were weighed at all; and so on.

However, be my memory in those matters right or wrong, it is but of little consequence. The one point that I do remember distinctly, and which I most gladly recall, is the very charming visit to "the most famous loch in Scotland," for which I was indebted to the friendly courtesy and kindness of two of her most famous anglers. In the hope of recalling such a pleasure, I so far accept Mr. Stewart's challenge that I will gladly, when the opportunity presents itself, fish a match with him in the same boat, and on the same loch, each to use his own flies tied by himself. This will be a better test of the merits of our respective flies than a burn-side match, in which so much more must depend upon the relative skill of the performers; and if I should lose, "as lose full well I may," I am sure that I cannot "take my death from a nobler hand."

H. Cholmondeley-Pennell.

WEYBRIDGE, *October 10.*

SIR—I observe in your paper of 15th inst. —which, owing to being from home I did not see sooner—a letter from Mr. Pennell, to which you will perhaps allow me a few final words in reply. I thought I had made my grounds of complaint sufficiently plain, but Mr. Pennell, who does not believe my statements, and has a remarkable knack of glorifying himself, will have it that I have paid him the compliment of getting in a rage at his arguments. The whole tenor of my letter made it sufficiently plain that I considered his arguments much more calculated to provoke merriment than wrath; and, so far as they are concerned, Mr. Pennell, as the *Scotsman* remarked, might safely be left to the mercy of his own arguments. But there are one or two other matters which I cannot pass over without remark. I do not intend discussing with Mr. Pennell whether he has borrowed or not—I gave the necessary references, and your readers can judge for themselves—but would merely remark in passing that upon the subject of Creeper and May-fly fishing he has not, as requested, informed us when he used these baits, and what he caught with them. His silence upon this point might lead to the supposition that he had seldom or never fished with them, as Mr. Pennell does not, as a rule, "hide his light under a bushel;" and if this supposition that he has little or no practical experience should be correct, and he did not borrow his information, most people would have some difficulty in making out how he got it at all.

Now, as to the title of my book, I must confess my ignorance. I was quite unaware of the existence of any other *Practical Angler*. In what Mr. Pennell would call this extreme want of erudition, however, I do not stand alone. Every angler to whom I have spoken was in the same position; so, I suppose, were the great majority of the readers of *The Field*; so, in August 1869, was Mr. Pennell himself. In that month Mr. Pennell mentioned to me that he intended writing a book upon angling, in which he meant to go in extensively for general fishing, said I had *monopolised* the best title, and asked me if I thought *The General Angler* would be a good title for his. Perhaps Mr. Pennell will kindly inform us when he discovered the existence of *The Practical Angler*, published in 1843.

I charged Mr. Pennell with misrepresenting matters about an excursion to Lochleven. This, he correctly says, "appears the greatest stumbling-block of all," and the reason is plain enough. The other differences between us might be matters of opinion, but this is a matter of fact. Mr. Pennell, who appears generally to stick to his statements—or rather misstatements—but does not seem quite sure about his memory, seems to think there were three separate days, and that the trout were not weighed on the day he was beaten. There was just one evening's fishing, as I stated, and the following day till about four o'clock; and the occupant of the boat who beat Mr. Pennell in the proportion of something like four to one weighed his take, because it was the best he ever got on the loch—26 lbs. Mr. Pennell and the other occupant did not weigh, not having much to weigh. It is quite common for anglers on Lochleven who have got little not to weigh; for instance, Mr. Pennell was the only one who weighed his fish on the previous evening.

Mr. Pennell says that he "did not violate the canons of courtesy." If putting words into your companions' mouths which they never used, misrepresenting the facts of the case, and upon this accusing your two companions in print of being the victims of local prejudices, be not violating the canons of courtesy, then our ideas of courtesy on this side the Tweed need modernising as much as our principles of angling.

Mr. Pennell appropriately reserves a crowning absurdity for the conclusion of his last letter, when, in answer to a challenge to test the merits of up and down stream fishing, he accepts it so far as to test the merits of his flies by a day's fishing on a loch where neither flies nor fishing matter much. It would occur to any one but Mr. Pennell that both flies and fishing would be much better tested on some stream where the trout are wary, and where great care is required in the selection of flies, and great skill in the using of them. His reason for changing from stream to loch is that it requires more skill on a stream, or, as he himself puts it, "a burn- side match, in which so much more must depend upon the individual skill of the performers."

When I suggested in my last that the reason why Mr. Pennell had not succeeded in up-stream fishing was want of skill, I had an idea I was pretty near the mark, but was certainly not prepared for a confession of the same from him; but, since he does not consider himself good enough, I am quite willing to allow him to fish by deputy, and upon flies I will give him his own way (he can tie the flies of the one party, and I will tie those of the other) ; and surely he can find among the great majority of anglers who keep him company one to do battle in his behalf. I thank you for your insertion of my last letter on this subject, and hope that next time I address you it may be on a more agreeable topic.

W. C. Stewart.

EDINBURGH, *October 22.*

SIR—From his letter of October 26 it seems that Mr. Stewart is very far from "pleased" with my book, *The Modern Practical Angler*; and this time his wrath is somewhat more intelligible. It must doubtless be not a little irritating, when a man has gratuitously provoked a personal controversy, to find himself thrown hopelessly on his back at every one of his intended standpoints.

Mr. Stewart twits his antagonist with copying the pattern of his hook. His antagonist mildly replies that, after careful search, no such pattern can be found anywhere in Mr. Stewart's writings; in fact, that Mr.

Stewart has not, and never had, any "pattern of hook" whatever, from which to copy.

Mr. Stewart taxes his opponent with plagiarising his worm-tackle, and misrepresenting it for his own purposes. His opponent gently refers to chapter and verse where he has published a facsimile of Mr. Stewart's tackle, and accorded to its author the entire credit of the invention.

Mr. Stewart charges his adversary with appropriating the title of his book; and his adversary blandly retorts that "Mr. Stewart's title" is not Mr. Stewart's at all, but somebody else's, from whom Mr. Stewart has bodily appropriated, whilst at the same time falsifying it.

Finally, Mr. Stewart attributes his competitor's success in beating him on a particular occasion to "chance," and the publishing of the fact (N.B., without names or dates) to "want of courtesy;" to which his competitor rejoins, still with perfect suavity, that whatever personal publicity had occurred in the matter had been given wholly by Mr. Stewart himself—that it was perfectly true that he did happen to beat Mr. Stewart on the occasion in question—and further, that he will have pleasure in backing himself to do the same thing again.

All this, I say, must naturally have been irritating to Mr. Stewart, who has from the outset been some-how rather exercised in his temper; for though I wished, for the sake of former acquaintance, to do my "spiriting as gently" as possible—a courtesy which, I regret to observe, has been wasted on my opponent, who does not seem to have any eye for what are called the "amenities of literature"—still facts are facts, and sometimes cannot but be sadly unpalatable, however politely they may be stated. It is not to be wondered at, therefore, that in his last letter Mr. Stewart should endeavour, by stirring up a great cloud of verbal dust, and executing the manœuvre known as "holding and spurring," to mystify the direct issues which he originally raised, and thus to ride off with some show at least of dignity.

I gladly help to make a bridge for a flying foe, and forbear to press him further by commenting, as I rnight, upon the somewhat peculiar notions of courtesy and modesty which have prompted Mr. Stewart not once, but a dozen times during this correspondence to attribute to me a want of literary good faith, and of angling skill as compared with his own, for which there is an utter absence of justification in our relative antecedents, literary or piscatorial. Nor do I care to notice, except perhaps by a passing smile, the comical tone suggestive somehow of canes and pedagogues in which he has thought fit to catechise me as to the extent of my experience and qualifications in "creeper fishing," "May-fly fishing," "up-stream fishing," and what not. Mr. Stewart is very welcome to his own opinion (however erroneous) on these points, as I am unconscious of meditating any immediate application to him for an angling diploma.

In the same way I abstain from amplifying what I have already written with regard to Mr. Stewart's challenges to fish a match—always by deputy be it observed—either against myself or a friend, on a Scotch burn-side. Such a contest would prove nothing, and convince nobody. Enough that I am prepared, as I have stated, to back my rod against Mr. Stewart's in a repetition of the only match, if it can be called such, that has been practically in question during this controversy, and the accuracy of my account of which he has disputed. But no "deputies," *bien entendu*. As they say on the turf, "owners up."

I must apologise for this (last I hope) trespass on your courtesy in these merely personal matters, of which your readers must long ere this be as weary as I am; and, wishing Mr. Stewart a more manageable theme and a less unmanageable opponent for his next controversial début, I am, etc.,

H. Cholmondeley-Pennell.

WEYBRIDGE, *November 1.*

[We do not see the possible use of permitting this controversy to continue, and therefore we now close it.—ED.]

When I announced in my last letter that I did not intend writing again to *The Field*, I by no means intended that Mr. Pennell was to be allowed to ride off in triumph. I made the announcement with the view, as it were, of unearthing Mr. Pennell, and getting him to show his true colours. Any one can see the difference in style between his first two letters and his last, though few would have expected that when he thought there was to be no further castigation, he would have indulged in such an astounding amount of assertion and impertinence. Assertion is not argument, and impertinence is not proof; and as I have no intention of following his lead in this way, I shall answer his letter in detail.

"Facts are facts," says Mr. Pennell; and with Pennellian inconsistency commences his letter with a gross misstatement of fact, by accusing me of having gratuitously provoked the controversy. He really must suppose his readers very defective in memory, if he suppose they have already forgotten that it was in answer to a personal attack by him in *The Field* I first wrote a reply.

By looking at page 47 of *The Practical Angler*, Mr. Pennell will find the pattern of hook which I recommend, and also the passage from which I accuse him of having borrowed the ideas upon which he has constructed the Pennell hook; "the result of some thought and experiment." I got hooks made after that pattern for my own use, but—for reasons which Mr. Pennell cannot be expected to understand—did not think of calling them Stewart. I did not accuse Mr. Pennell of plagiarising my worm-tackle. I said that he had introduced a new worm-tackle by reducing the three-hook tackle, which usually goes by my name, to two, and making the hooks a little larger. I distinctly charged Mr. Pennell with appropriating the title of my book, and charge him with it still. When Mr. Pennell called his book *The Modern Practical Angler*, he did not know of the existence of any other *Practical Angler* but mine; and though his subsequent discovery may lessen the legal guilt, it has no effect upon the moral bearings of the question, and in no degree diminishes the shabbiness of Mr. Pennell's conduct to me.

I certainly did attribute Mr. Pennell's catching seven trout to my six in two hours' evening fishing to chance, and cannot possibly see why he should find fault with that, when I also attributed my catching 26 lbs. weight to his about 6 lbs. in a whole day's fishing next day to chance also. Whether there is a want of both honesty and courtesy in Mr. Pennell's statement of his Lochleven excursion, the reader can judge for himself. *My statement is correct, and I have witnesses to prove it.*

Mr. Pennell charges me with having no eye

for the amenities of literature. If the amenities of literature mean something like the following letter, which I select from his own correspondence, we are likely to differ upon this point also; and that the reader may thoroughly understand the matter, I give the letter which drew forth this *gentlemanly and extremely argumentative reply.*

Fly-Fishing Up and Down stream

Sir—Mr. Pennell's letter in reply to Mr. Stewart strikes me as being, in reference to the main point under discussion, singularly feeble and evasive. One would have thought that a letter so exhaustive on this point as Mr. Stewart's would not have been answered by Mr. Pennell, having "nothing to add to his arguments of September 24." The only possible inference is that, as regards the *casus belli*, Mr. Pennell is judiciously abandoning an untenable position.

May I ask Mr. Pennell if he seriously contends that a fish can see behind as well as he can see before and why he sanctions fishing up in "shallow waters with a sun and no ripple on them?" or how a stream should be fished with a rapid "draw" on, but no ripple?

Formerly a down-stream fisher myself, I have been for many years a convert to a great extent to Mr.

Stewart's plan, and have at least half-a-dozen friends (some of them crack hands) who have changed their *modus operandi* with marked success.

Applied to sea-trout fishing, when a river is low and clear I will undertake to kill three fish to Mr. Pennell's one. In a medium-sized water my bag would be three to his two. In a big water I readily concede that fishing down is preferable, and always do so. Wading is much easier, consequently more ground is covered.

Mr. Francis has written excellent sense upon this subject, and, although books alone will never make anglers, I should recommend all who want a wrinkle or two about up and down stream fishing to read his concisely-stated remarks.

LILLYHOLME.

SOUTHPORT, *October 17.*

FLY-FISHING UP STREAM

SIR—Your correspondent, signing himself "Lillyholme," has thought it necessary to add to the already voluminous correspondence which you have published on the up or down stream fishing, his principal object being apparently to take me to task for my reticence in replying to the numerous observations which have been made on the propositions contained in my article of the 24th of September on this subject. I really ought to feel very grateful to "Lillyholme" for being so good as to instruct me how to conduct my correspondence. Let me prove my gratitude by making in his case an exception to my general rule of passing *sub silentio* the attacks of anonymous writers, and I select with the more pleasure this mode of discharging my obligations to your correspondent, inasmuch as his letter furnishes a very fair illustration of one of the principal reasons of my reticence in this matter—viz. the total irrelevancy of most of the arguments used by my critics. "Lillyholme," who is doubtless the victim of that very prevalent modern disease, the "itch for writing," evidently does not understand how any one can resist an opportunity for rushing into print, or so far possess his argument in patience as to decline unnecessary weekly recapitulations and taxes on space which would be otherwise better occupied.

Now, I repeat that my original propositions—which were neither crude nor hasty productions, but the result of much thought and consideration—have never been fairly met or logically controverted, my opponents having usually adopted the very convenient mode of argument ungallantly attributed by a satirist to the softer sex—

She'll argue with you a whole summer's day,
And she'll refute—whatever you don't *say!*

I have noticed that "Lillyholme's" letter is a very fair instance of this kind of logic. Let me point out to him why I think so, taking sentences of his letter *seriatim*.

1st sentence. Mr. Pennell declines "to add to his arguments of the 24th Sept.;"—*therefore,* it is evident that he "is judiciously abandoning an untenable position."

2d sentence. Mr. Pennell having stated that "the position of the eye of a trout is such as to enable him to see much more readily anything above or on one side than in front of him" —"Lillyholme" begs to "ask Mr. Pennell if he seriously contends that a fish can see behind as well as he can before."

3d sentence. "And why he sanctions fishing up in shallow waters with a sun and no ripple on them?"—the sense of which question (having reference to juxtaposition and to my argument) appears to be about equal to that of the celebrated rigmarole, "What! no soap? So he died, and she very imprudently married the barber."

The remainder of "Lillyholme's" letter consists of a *mélange* of small personalities, and great trumpet-blowings of his own many angling achievements *in posse*, and of how many more big fish he, the critic, could catch, under various conditions of wind and water, than I, his unfortunate author—an enumeration in which (must I acknowledge it to my confusion?) I find myself literally nowhere.

Perhaps "Lillyholme" will now have some glimmering why I do not think it necessary to be perpetually armed *cap-à-pie*, and ready to rush into conflict with every adventurous cavalier, known or unknown, who may wish to splinter lances under the safe shield of a *nom de plume*; and if this letter should act in future abatement of the annoyance (which I observe I am not singular in expressing) of illogical as well as irresponsible criticism, the result apparently of mere love of contradiction, poor "Lillyholme" of Southport will not have been gibbeted in vain.

H. Cholmondeley-Pennell.

Mr. Pennell is again in error when he says I attributed to him a want of angling skill as compared with my own. Mr. Pennell attributed want of skill to himself, when he declined to fish a match in a stream because "more must depend upon the relative skill of the performers." I have never in the whole correspondence said a single word about myself as an angler; a fact of which he is aware, for he accuses me of always offering to fish by deputy. When I offered to bring a person to catch 2 lbs. weight for Mr. Pennell's 1 lb., I certainly intended to fish myself; and if that is his only objection to the match, by all means let us have the up or down stream question practically tested, "owners up," as he expresses it ; and I by no means limit it to a Scotch burn, but will fish in any stream in England of the kind described. As for the match proving nothing and convincing nobody, I differ from that conclusion entirely; it would prove Mr. Pennell's flies useless, and his method of using them ridiculous. I thought it quite impossible that any one who knew anything of fly-fishing in clear water could write such nonsense as he has done. It seems, however, that there are some anglers who have courage to try anything new, however ridiculous, and at least one old angler equipped himself with some of the typical flies. Of course he fell a victim to his temerity, but let him speak for himself.

Mr. Pennell on Fly-Fishing.

Sir—Most men who are fond of a sport like reading the experiences of others on that subject, and books on hunting and shooting contain ideas tolerably similar to those held by the rest of the hunting and shooting world. But writers on fishing (fly-fishing especially) seem to try how far they can set aside all acknowledged theories.

I read a book on fishing by Mr. Pennell some short time ago that out-herods Herod in this respect. I have been a fisherman with fly for twenty years, and during the last five years have fished, I believe, as much as any man in England, and my experience is that fish take the artificial fly for the natural one. I see no difficulty in proving this by the water-side, but wish to say a word with regard to the three curious devices that Mr. Pennell in the above work recommends as typical flies.

Having procured some of different sizes (from one of his accredited agents), I tried them for grayling on three rivers—the Teme, Lugg, and Arrow in this manner:—I made up a cast, with one of the typical flies as stretcher and another as drop, and between these I put on a third fly, in imitation of the one the fish were then taking. I killed a fair amount of fish each day, but every single fish on the imitation of the natural fly, not getting one rise to any of the three flies of Mr. Pennell's pattern.

There is a mention made in the book of Mr. Pennell's personal experience of the Leintwardine water on the Teme, although no statement of any take of fish by him there. I should like to know whether he ever killed any grayling of a takeable size on that water, using only his own three flies. I do not believe they would kill either brown trout or grayling on any river in the world that throws up any insect life, and even for lake fishing and white trout they could not hold their own with the ones generally used. The three salmon flies recommended in the book are all of one sort. Any salmon fisherman, if restricted to that number, could pick out of his book three more adapted to different conditions of water. I think most fishermen will agree with me that it is rather presumptuous in Mr. Pennell to write epitaphs, as he says, on the system of fly-fishing that our experience has proved right.

DRAGOON.

Inconvenient questions Mr. Pennell declines to answer, and passes by with a few slang expressions; and when charged with borrowing without leave a whole chapter on May-fly fishing, etc., seems to think I am most unreasonable in complaining of his conduct, because he has always spoken in praise of my book, and recommended his readers to study certain portions of it. I do not suppose that Mr. Pennell would have borrowed unless he had approved; but if every one who plagiarises is to be held guiltless on these principles, a little further application of them would do away with the crime of theft altogether, as no one ever steals unless he admires the article. Had Mr. Pennell asked permission to make use of any portion of *The Practical Angler*, he would have been as welcome to it as on a former occasion.

It is quite as well Mr. Pennell has no *immediate* intention of applying to me for an angling diploma, for he would most assuredly be plucked in his preliminary examination; but, if he will study *The Practical Angler* carefully, and practise the precepts therein contained, there is no saying but something might be done in this way ultimately.

I feel duly grateful to Mr. Pennell for his kind wish that I may meet with a more manageable theme and a less unmanageable opponent for my next controversial *début*; but I would "meekly" point out to him that I cannot make a *début* in controversy twice, and in return would "blandly" suggest to him that, when he again indulges in controversy, it might be expedient to confine himself to the use of words of which he understands the meaning. I am, however, quite pleased with my opponent. Not being accustomed to writing, it is, I suppose, as well for me that I have had a feeble antagonist, with a hopeless cause, to commence with; and it is so easy to answer one like Mr. Pennell, who lays himself so delightfully open to attack—who, in fact, rushes "with bare bosom on the spear."

In the preface to his book Mr. Pennell challenged the opinion of what he called the general parliament of anglers. I suppose the general parliament of anglers may be considered pretty fairly represented by the readers of *The Field* newspaper, and these in turn by the writers to that paper. Well, letter after letter appeared, but no writer had a single word to say in defence of Mr. Pennell's theories on flies. The verdict which the general parliament of anglers has unanimously pronounced against him he proceeds to reserve in his own favour, and with the most amusing gravity states generally what a giant in controversy he (Mr. Pennell) is, and how careful any one should be of attempting to break a lance with him—how he has gibbeted this one, thrown another hopelessly on his back, and generally routed all his foes. Ill-natured people might remark that all this might have come better from a neutral party or a friend than from Mr. Pennell himself; but then—to borrow the expression which this stickler for the amenities of literature used to "Lillyholme"—what could poor Pennell do? the neutrals were all against him, and his friends—if he has any—probably thought it would be a work of supererogation to say anything in praise of a person so eminently qualified to act as his own trumpeter.

One reviewer remarked that he hoped in the next edition of Mr. Pennell's book to see it better, which Mr. Pennell can easily accomplish by deleting a little more of what is original, and substituting borrowed information. However, to be done with *The Modern Practical Angler*:—

> *"Hope, like the glimmering taper's light,*
> *Adorns and cheers the way;*
> *And still, as darker grows the night,*
> *Emits a brighter ray."*

And, even in this compound of plagiarism, absurdity, and self-conceit, the reader may discover one gleam of comfort, which he will find in the preface, where Mr. Pennell announces he has "probably addressed an angling audience for the last time."

The up or down stream question having been thoroughly discussed—if it can be called a discussion, with about a score of evidently able anglers arguing and stating experiences on one side, and Mr. Pennell asserting on the other—the general opinion may be summed up as follows: That in all small streams it is absolutely necessary to fish up. That in medium-sized streams, unless when large and discoloured, it is much better to fish up; but that in large streams, where it is almost impossible to wade up, more fish may be taken by fishing down, because more water can be covered. That these are exactly the views embodied in *"The Practical Angler*, or the Art of Trout-fishing, more particularly applied to Clear Water," the following quotations will show:—

"When the water is of a dark colour, it conceals the angler from view, and disguises his tackle, and so he meets with fair sport. If the body of water, though clear, is sufficiently large to conceal him from the sight of the trout, as in Tweed, Tay, and other first-class streams, he may still meet with tolerable success. But in all our small rivers and waters, when they are low and clear, not one angler out of twenty meets with much sport, and the reason of it is, because the clearness of the water either allows the trout to see him, or enables them to detect the artificial nature of his lure; and to meet these difficulties as far as possible, is the great object to be aimed at in fly-fishing.

"The great error of fly-fishing, as usually practised, and as recommended to be practised by books, is that the angler fishes down stream, whereas he should fish up.

"We believe we are not beyond the mark in stating that ninety-nine anglers out of a hundred fish down with the artificial fly; they never think of fishing in any other way, and never dream of attributing their want of success to it. Yet we are prepared to prove,

A CAUTION TO ANGLERS

both in theory and practice, that this is the greatest reason of their want of success in clear waters. In all our angling excursions we have only met one or two amateurs, and a few professionals, who fished up stream with the fly, and used it in a really artistic manner. If the wind is blowing up, anglers will occasionally fish up the pools—(as for fishing up a strong stream they never think of it)—but even then they do not do it properly, and meet with little better success than if they had followed their usual method. They will also, if going to some place up a river, walk up, not fish up to it—their plan being to go to the top of a pool, and then fish it down, never casting their line above them at all.

"We shall now mention in detail the advantages of fishing up, in order to show its superiority over the old method.

"The first and greatest advantage is, that the angler is unseen by the trout. Trout, as is well known, keep their heads up stream; they cannot remain stationary in any other position. This being the case, they see objects above and on both sides of them, but cannot discern anything behind them; so that the angler fishing down will be seen by them twenty yards off, whereas the angler fishing up will be unseen, although he be but a few yards in their rear. The advantages of this it is impossible to over-estimate. No creatures are more easily scared than trout; if they see any object moving on the river's bank, they run into deep water, or beneath banks and stones, from which they will not stir for some time. A bird flying across the water, or the shadow of a rod, will sometimes alarm them; and nothing connected with angling is more certain than this, that if the trout see the angler they will not take his lure. He may ply his minnow in the most captivating manner, may throw his worm with consummate skill, or make his flies light softly as a gossamer—all will be unavailing if he is seen by his intended victim.

"The next advantage of fishing up we shall notice, is the much greater probability of hooking a trout when it rises. In angling down stream, if a trout rises and the angler strikes, he runs a great risk of pulling the flies straight out of its mouth; whereas, in fishing up, its back is to him, and he has every chance of bringing the hook into contact with its jaws. This, although it may not seem of great importance to the uninitiated, tells considerably when the contents of the basket come to be examined at the close of the day's sport; indeed no angler would believe the difference unless he himself proved it.

"Another advantage of fishing up is, that it does not disturb the water so much. Let us suppose the angler is fishing down a fine pool. He, of course, commences at the top, the place where the best trout, and those most inclined to feed, invariably lie. After a few casts he hooks one, which immediately runs down, and by its vagaries, leaping in the air, and plunging in all directions, alarms all its neighbours, and it is ten to one if he gets another rise in that pool. Fishing up saves all this. The angler commences at the foot, and when he hooks a trout, pulls it down, and the remaining portions of the pool are undisturbed. This is a matter of great importance, and we have frequently, in small streams, taken a dozen trout out of a pool, from which, had we been fishing down, we could not possibly have got more than two or three.

"The last advantage of fishing up is, that by it the angler can much better adapt the motions of his flies to those of the natural insect. And here it may be mentioned as a rule, that the nearer the motions of the artificial flies resemble those of the natural ones under similar circumstances, the greater will be the prospects of success. Whatever trout take the artificial fly for, it is obvious they are much more likely to be deceived by a natural than by an unnatural motion.

"No method of angling can imitate the hovering flight of an insect along the surface of the water, now just touching it, then flying a short distance, and so on; and for the angler to attempt by any motion of his hand to give his flies a living appearance is mere absurdity. The only moment when trout may mistake the angler's fly for a real one in its flight, is the moment it first touches the water; and in this respect fishing down possesses equal advantages with fishing up. But this is the only respect, and in order to illustrate this, we shall give a brief description of fly-fishing as usually practised down stream.

"The angler, then, we shall suppose, commences operations at the head of a pool or stream, and, throwing his flies as far as he can across from where he is standing, raises his rod and brings them gradually to his own side of the water. He then steps down a yard or two, repeats the process, and so on. Having dismissed the idea that the angler can imitate the flight of a living fly along the surface of the water, we must suppose that trout take the artificial fly for a dead one, or one which has fairly got into the stream and lost all power of resisting. A feeble motion of the wings or legs would be the only attempt at escape which a live fly in such a case could make. What then must be the astonishment of the trout, when they see the tiny insect which they are accustomed to seize as it is carried by the current towards them, crossing the stream with the strength and agility of an otter? Is it not much more natural to throw the flies up, and let them come gently down as any real insect would do?

"In addition to drawing their flies across the

stream, some anglers practise what is called playing their flies, which is done by a jerking motion of the wrist, which imparts a similar motion to the fly. Their object in doing this is to create an appearance of life, and thus render their flies more attractive. An appearance of life is certainly a great temptation to a trout, but it may be much better accomplished by dressing the flies of soft materials, which the water can agitate, and thus create a natural motion of the legs or wings of the fly, than by dragging them by jumps of a foot at a time across and up a roaring stream. Trout are not accustomed to see small insects making such gigantic efforts at escape, and therefore it is calculated to awaken their suspicions.

"We believe that all fly-fishers fishing down must have noticed that, apart from the moment of alighting, they get more rises for the first few yards of their flies' course than in the whole of the remainder; and that when their flies fairly breast the stream they seldom get a rise at all. The reason of this is clear—: for the first few feet after the angler throws his flies across the stream they swim with the current; the moment, however, he begins to describe his semi-circle across the water, they present an unnatural appearance, which the trout view with distrust. Experienced fly-fishers, following the old method, who have observed this, and are aware of the great importance of the moment their flies alight, cast very frequently, only allowing their flies to float down a few feet, when they throw again. We have seen some Tweedside adepts fill capital baskets in this way; but, as we have before stated, it will only succeed when the water is coloured, or when there is a body of clear water sufficiently large to conceal the angler from view."

I mention, subsequently, that when wading is an objection, the angler should fish down; and also, "The only circumstance in which fishing down has the advantage of fishing up, is when the water is so dark or deep that the fish would not see, or if they did see, would not have time to seize the flies, unless they moved at a slower rate than the stream."

In my first letter, I accused Mr. Pennell of quoting a few lines without giving the context, so I give quotation and context here.

"We must confess, however, that fishing up stream with fly has not been adopted by a large portion of the angling community, and that for various reasons. In spite of the strong manner in which we cautioned our readers about the difficulties of fishing up stream, numbers who read the arguments for it, and were struck with the soundness of the theory, thought they saw at a glance the cause of their previous want of success, and that in future the result would be different. Having equipped themselves à la *Practical*

Angler, and even taken a copy of that excellent work in their pockets, they started with high hopes on their new career, but the result was not different, and after one or two trials with no better success, not a few have condemned fishing up stream as erroneous and ourselves as impostors; though we imagine the fault lies with themselves. We have met with anglers fishing down stream—and this is no supposititious case, but one which we have seen over and over again—with a copy of this volume in their pockets, who complained that they had got everything herein recommended, and were getting no sport. On pointing out to them that there was one important mistake they were committing, in fishing down stream instead of up, they stated that when they came to a pool they fished it up—that is to say, they first walked down the pool and showed themselves to the trout, and then commenced to fish for them.

> " ' *The trout within yon wimplin' burn*
> *Glides swift, a silver dart;*
> *And, safe beneath the shady thorn,*
> *Defies the angler's art.*' "

"John Younger objects to this as incorrect, but we rather think that Burns is right and the angler wrong; as it is evident the poet alludes to a trout that has caught sight of the angler, and safe he is, at least *pro tem.*, as our pupils who first frighten the fish by walking down a pool-side, and then fish up it, will find to their cost.

"Others object to fishing up stream, as requiring too frequent casting, being too fatiguing, and because they have been accustomed to fish down, and would prefer fishing in that way, even though they do not catch so many trout. If any angler prefers catching five pounds weight of trout fishing down stream, to ten pounds weight fishing up, we may wonder at his taste, but it is no concern of ours. Our duty is to point out how most trout can be captured in a given time; and that is by fishing up stream, and such is now the method adopted by all the best fly-fishers of the day.

"Those anglers who have adopted fishing up stream are principally those who were adepts in the old system, and who were possessed of all the nicety in casting, and other knowledge so essential to successful up-stream fishing."

Since I last published upon angling, there has been a marked decrease in the number of trout in most of the border streams, and it is now—unless weather and water are exceptionally favourable—a very hard day's work to make even a decent basket; and it becomes a subject worthy of the serious consideration of all anglers, to see if anything can be done to improve the state of matters, or at anyrate, prevent them from getting worse; for if the trout-fishing falls off as much during the next ten years as it has done during the last ten, it will hardly be worth while going to the water-side at all. The causes that have occasioned this are no doubt various, and amongst the minor ones may be mentioned the increase of manufactories, and the quantity of lime put upon the land. To this latter cause is probably owing the almost total disappearance of minnows from Tweed and some other streams, and, if injurious to minnows, it must be the same in some degree to young trout. As, however, trout are getting fewer in number in streams where manufactories have not yet reached, and where lime is comparatively little used, the main cause must be looked for elsewhere. There are also undoubtedly a great many trout taken by netting, but there is no evidence that netting is more common now than it was fifteen years ago; the precautions taken to prevent it are much greater, and, if there is any difference, it seems probable that there are fewer trout killed by the net than formerly. The great cause of the diminution I believe to be over-fishing with the rod; there are in fact too many anglers, or they fish too much. Land will only grow a certain quantity of grain, or maintain a certain number of cattle or sheep, and in like manner a stream can only rear and maintain a certain quantity of trout, and unless a sufficient stock is left to breed from, it is evident that gradual decrease must be the result; and sooner or later the conviction will be forced upon anglers that they must not kill so many trout. The remedy which at once suggests itself is, that there should be a close-time for trout. There is a close-time for salmon, also for oysters; in fact, in regard to this latter fish, Government has been compelled, in addition to the close-time, to make regulations as to size, etc., in order to prevent proprietors from exterminating their own property. Sea-gulls have even been put under the protection of law, and there seems no valid reason why trout a fish that affords healthful amusement to a greater number, than any other fish that swims, or any bird that flies, should not also be put under the protection of the law.

The period of close-time I should propose to be those months when trout are out of condition, say roundly from the middle of October to the middle of March, the time being varied according to the nature of the stream or district. If the stream or district is early, the close-time should commence sooner and terminate sooner; and, if the stream or district is late, the reverse. Some people who are not acquainted with the real state of matters may be of opinion that there are not many trout killed during the months of the proposed close-time; but if any one holding such an opinion will pay a visit to Tweed in the end of October or November, when the river is in flood, he will soon be convinced of the contrary. Trout are more easily taken in a flooded water at that season of the year than any other, and he will find every pool suitable for the purpose literally clad with anglers, following one another down at intervals of a few yards, and, when they reach the bottom of the pool, returning again to the top, and this process goes on so regularly and so continuously, that—and this is no exaggeration—I have seen two broad footpaths marked on the green bank with the regularity of a pair of rails. Of course all the parties engaged are nominally fishing with worm, but the real slaughter is done with salmon-roe. The reader will of course say salmon-roe fishing is illegal; what of that? it is just as much fished with as ever, and is cured on Tweed and tributaries by the hundredweight. All the salmon-roe cured is used, and yet I have never, since the Act was passed, seen a single conviction for using salmon-roe, or being found with it in possession. The Tweed Commissioners should, as a matter of course, look after this, but that existing but almost useless body probably have not sufficient means at their disposal, and certainly do not make the best use of the means they have, as they allow kelt-killing and parr-killing to go on under their very eyes, and *with the sanction of their bailiffs*. The trout killed in

October and November are almost all spawning fish, and, if they were left to deposit their ova, it would give a considerable increase in the number of trout in any stream where such practices go on.

The proposal for a close-time will, of course, meet with great opposition, especially from the principal offenders, but I would point out to all honest anglers, that, in what are usually called open waters, angling is *a privilege and not a right*, and if that privilege is not exercised in a fair and sportsmanlike way, proprietors may at any time take the matter into their own hands, and stop the public from fishing at all, and unless some steps are taken, such will be the result. Truth may be sometimes unpleasant, but it is nevertheless truth, and the fact—however painful the admission may be—is, that anglers as a class have less of the true spirit of sportsmen about them than the lovers of any other field sport. They will kill kelts, kill par, fish with salmon-roe, or break the law in any way, if they think they can get off without detection, and, like the proprietors of oyster-fisheries, salmon-fisheries, etc., must be protected against themselves.

The formation of Angling Associations should also be encouraged, who would collect funds, and see that the existing laws were fairly carried out by the members; and if any one, not a member of such association, were caught fishing illegally, any proprietor would doubtless grant an interdict against his fishing again.

The question will of course arise, What is to be done with a river like the Clyde, which contains grayling, a fish which is in its prime when trout are out of condition? Holding the views already mentioned about the honesty of a certain class of anglers, I would make no exception in favour of allowing anglers to fish grayling in the Clyde. The anglers who fish at that season are of the very worst sort, and if allowed to fish grayling, there are very few who would be inclined to lay odds, that, in the very probable event of their catching more trout than grayling, they would return the trout to the river. Besides, the cultivation of grayling should not be encouraged; they are an inferior fish to trout; they live upon the same sort of food as trout, and, as a river only supplies a certain quantity of feeding, if there are more grayling there must be fewer trout. They are also in season at a time of year when angling is shorn of almost all its charms.

Fifth Edition, revised and enlarged, Price 3s. 6d.

THE PRACTICAL ANGLER,

OR

THE ART OF TROUT-FISHING

MORE PARTICULARLY APPLIED
TO CLEAR WATER.

BY W. C. STEWART.

———◆———

OPINIONS OF THE PRESS.

BLACKWOOD'S MAGAZINE.

"Mr. Stewart has the reputation of being a most successful angler, and his fame is on many waters. Therefore, holding the views which we have already expressed touching the general selfishness of the fraternity, we cannot too much admire his single-heartedness in com-piling a work which, if attended to, must transmute the veriest tyro into a tolerably prosperous fisherman. We suspect that some who now rank as his rivals will barely thank him for his revelations, on the score that it is not expedient either to multiply the number of rods, or to divulge secrets which must tend to a considerable thinning of the streams. They, the adepts, believe themselves to constitute a high and worshipful piscatory lodge, with mysteries peculiar to their degree; and they may not altogether approve of the extreme liberality of their excellent brother in opening the eyes of the uninitiated. However, they may comfort themselves with the reflection that darkness rather than light is the deliberate choice of the million. The best teaching in the world is thrown

A CAUTION TO ANGLERS

away upon stupidity and self-conceit; and that not only in ethics, but in such practical matters as angling. . . . One special recommendation of this book as an angling treatise is, the clearness with which Mr. Stewart lays down his positions, and the care which he has bestowed on the proof. He does not content himself with merely giving directions; he explains, and always lucidly, why such directions are given.

BELL'S LIFE IN LONDON.

"Without hesitation we pronounce this little treatise the best we have ever read on angling for trout with the artificial fly, worm, minnow, and other baits. It is written with most minute care by an angler of fifteen years' constant practice, of great and varied observation, unprejudiced by egotistical theory, of sound judgment, and whose whole some knowledge of the habits of trout renders all that he says about the best modes of capturing entitled to the utmost confidence. . . . Every young fly-fisher, desirous of becoming proficient in by far the pleasantest and best branch of the angling art, should study the excellent and manifold maxims laid down in this most valuable little treatise. The tyro that does may rest assured that he is in his right path, following a practical, experienced, clever, and conscientious guide."

ILLUSTRATED LONDON NEWS.

"That patient class of British sportsmen for whom the Blink-bonnys and the Skirmishers of the turf live and race in vain, and whose hearts are not with the Kestrels or the Americas on the waters of the Solent, or in the tents of the scorers at Lord's or Kennington Oval, but continue to believe, summer after summer, in the spirit of the old song—

> 'Oh! the gallant fisher's life,
> It is the best of any!'

will take this terse little book to their bosom, and make it the companion of many a river-side pilgrimage. Its aim is not to give any highly-tinted dissertation on the joys of angling, or to produce a series of mental pictures of its most favoured haunts. Alas, for the silver trout! the author had a much more practical and deadly object in view ; and although the gentle craft have had teachers, and to spare, since their quaint old Isaak wrote, it was reserved for him to prove that almost, if not quite, as good sport may be had in clear water as in coloured.

"Mr. Stewart brings a large stock of enthusiasm, and fifteen years practice, to his work. He has gleaned for his letterpress, and his hook and bait illustrations, from nearly all the first amateurs and professional anglers of the day, and exchanged minds with Jamie Baillie, the veritable senior wrangler of fly-fishing in Scotland. Delightful as it may be to a beginner to wander, rod in hand, along the banks of some river in May or June, among meadows rich with the daisy and the cowslip, or to contemplate nature in her grander, but not less beautiful aspect, on the rocky heather-clad verge of a Highland stream—the pleasures of the day always bear some proportion to the weight of the basket brought home; and the finest scenery influences are but an indifferent compensation for an empty creel.

"By carefully studying the precepts so pithily and pleasantly enunciated here, no tyro need despair, after he has undergone his probation, of becoming a practical angler; and even those who worthily aspire to that distinction already, and have acquired the necessary neatness of hand and quickness of eye, may have their observation not a little sharpened and their prejudices sapped. The treatise is remarkably complete in all the details of the trout-fishing art. Fresh-water trout—the causes of their decrease, the season when they are in highest condition, and every phase of their natural history—claim a chapter. All the minutiae of an angler's equipment are gone into with quite a Gerard-Dow minuteness, and so on to artificial fly-fishing, flies,

A CAUTION TO ANGLERS

fly-dressing, May-fly fishing, and trouting with the fly. Angling with the worm, which he considers to possess one very solid advantage over fly in the superior size of the trout caught, is also copiously handled, as well as minnow and parr-tail baits. Loch-fishing, in which the accomplished angler and the tyro are most upon a par, has, nevertheless no small charm in his eyes; and his book is appropriately concluded by some precepts on 'the best means of filling a basket in May, June, July, August, and September.' The author has shown, to quote the late Mr. Barnes, 'lots of grapple' in dealing with his subject; and we trust that his readers may be able to act up to the spirit of the phrase, and remember his advice when they feel the thrilling nibble, and have to go gallantly into action at a moment's notice with a Highland *Salmo ferox* in the approaching summer."

SATURDAY REVIEW.

"Mr. Stewart's book, *The Practical Angler*, entirely fulfils its title. The author, who is said to be the -best fisherman in Scotland, has an object, and keeps it steadily in view it—is to teach the art of killing trout in clear water. He says, and with entire truth, that anybody can kill fish in a coloured stream. His cardinal point of faith is to fish up-stream. Here is true wisdom. A trout lies up-stream—his work is to take flies and food floating down-stream. In fishing up-stream you are behind your fish, and, great as are the capacities of a fish's eyes, it stands to reason that the angler at his tail has more chance of being undiscovered than if he charges his enemy en face. Next comes the advantage that in striking a fish your chances are greater in striking against him than in snatching from him. And when you have struck a fish you pull him into water that you have already fished over—you pull him down stream, leaving all the water above you undisturbed. What is meant by fly-fishing? Of course the object is to deceive the trout into the belief that he sees a real live fly. Which is most likely to deceive him—a fly cast above him and gently floating down to him, or one cast in the ordinary fashion, and madly crossing the stream at eccentric angles and with galvanised jerks? Real insects never cross a stream, driving up against the current by superhuman, not to say superinsectine, leaps and plunges. Fish may be caught by flies drawn up and across the stream; but nature's way is the best, and that floats flies down stream. Of course in dark and coloured waters the difference is less important; but Mr. Stewart's lesson is how to kill trout in clear water. And we heartily subscribe to his canons—with the modification that casting up stream is not to be always straight up, but diagonally, going over the whole water, but still casting upwards. Another very sensible observation of Mr. Stewart is that the colour of a fly is not half so important as the way in which it is made to fall and float on the water. A small fly and clear gut are *sine quibus non*; and the thing to aim at is the appearance of life, not colour, in your artificial bait. A more practical, sound, sensible, and unpretending book we never read, and we recommend it without abatement or qualification."

SCOTSMAN.

"This book is the probable inauguration of a new era in the art of angling. . . . Although the angler's library is already a pretty full one, each half-century for the last three hundred years having produced one or more pleasant and useful additions to it, we have no hesitation in saying that it cannot be complete without this little volume. Nowhere that we know of in the same compass, or indeed in any compass, is there so much valuable practical instruction to the trout-fisher. Mr. Stewart indulges but little in those graces of composition through which some of our least useful angling-books are rendered the most charming to the reader, but crams every page with information, which, from its obvious accordance with common sense and sound theory, not less than from its being vouched for by an angler of large experience, and of a skill that has never yet been matched, commends itself as valuable even to the most sceptical and self-satisfied adept."

THE FIELD.

"The modest unpretending little volume before us is decidedly welcome. *The Practical Angler*—we like the title. We are prepared to find something practical in it, and thanks be, for once we are not deceived. It is practical in every sense of the word. . . . We can recommend this little book to tyros or anglers in the transition state of every grade and shade, and even the finished practitioner may find in it something worthy of notice."

JOHN BULL.

. . . . "But the author' needs no excuse, and has limited himself to no specialty. He has given us the very best hand-book of angling that we know of; and it is a material part of its merits that it occupies so small a compass; for most anglers, however they may affect a voluminous fishing-book, are disposed to cavil at prolixity in a treatise on this science. Short as it is, the work contains all that is needed, either for the fly at the one end of the machinery, or the angler at the other. How to make your fly, how to throw it; how to hook your fish, how to land it; all about your own habits and those of the trout, is told in a simple and sportsmanlike style. Mr. Stewart is the Colonel Hawker of fishing."

ADAM & CHARLES BLACK.

OTHER IMPORTANT FLY-FISHING BOOKS
AVAILABLE FROM
THE FLYFISHER'S CLASSIC LIBRARY

A Salmon Fisher's Odyssey – John Ashley-Cooper
The Flyfisher's Guide – G. C. Bainbridge
The Art of Fly Making – William Blacker
An Angler's Paradise – F. D. Barker
Brook & River Trouting – Edmonds and Lee
Flytyer's Masterclass – Oliver Edwards
The Book of the Salmon – Ephemera
Going Fishing – Negley Farson
Golden Days – Romilly Fedden
A Book on Angling – Francis Francis
Fly Fishing – Sir Edward Grey
An Angler's Autobiography – F. M. Halford
The House the Hardy Brothers Built – J. L. Hardy
A Summer on the Test – J. W. Hills
My Sporting Life – J. W. Hills
River Keeper – J. W. Hills
Autumns on the Spey – A. E. Knox
Salmon and Sea Trout – Sir Herbert Maxwell
Fly-Fishing: Some New Arts and Mysteries – J. C. Mottram
Fishing in Eden – William Nelson
Grayling Fishing – W. Carter Platts
The Book of the Grayling – T. E. Pritt
How to Dress Salmon Flies – T. E. Pryce-Tannatt
Rod and Line – Arthur Ransome
Flies for Snowdonia – Plu Eryri – William Roberts
The Frank Sawyer Omnibus – Frank Sawyer
Days and Nights of Salmon Fishing on the Tweed – W. Scrope
Nymph Fishing for Chalk Stream Trout – G. E. M. Skues
Silk, Fur and Feather: The Fly Dresser's Handbook – G. E. M. Skues
Side-lines, Side-lights and Reflections – G. E. M. Skues
The Way of a Trout with a Fly – G. E. M. Skues
The Practical Angler – W. C. Stewart
Jones's Guide to Norway – F. Tolfrey
Grayling and How to Catch Them – F. M. Walbran
The Rod and Line – H. Wheatley
River Angling for Salmon and Trout – J. Younger
Three in Norway by Two of Them

The Flyfisher's Classic Library – Coch-y-Bonddu Books
Machynlleth, Mid-Wales, SY20 8DG
Tel: 01654 702837
www.ffcl.com   www.anglebooks.com